FINDING ECSTASY

How Buenos Aires, a Brazilian, and the Blues Saved My Sex Life (and My Soul)

Copyright

Finding Ecstasy
How Buenos Aires, a Brazilian, and the Blues Saved My Sex Life (and My Soul)

Cover Design by Antonio Garcia Martin

Published by Duende Press

ISBN: 978-0-9915254-1-6

To Boris, for saying *hola* to me across the patio table.

TABLE OF CONTENTS

I
Leaving Home

1
What's My Fantasy?

"**WHAT IS YOUR** fantasy world like?"

"My fantasy world? Well, I've always dreamed I could fly."

"Hmm, that's a lovely dream, Rebecca, but I'm talking about your sexual fantasy world."

"Oh..." I knew every question was going to be related to sex—this was sex therapy, after all—but I couldn't bring myself to address the topic directly. I felt compelled to delay the inevitable and answer each question in a deliberately roundabout manner. I sat in the corner of a floral-patterned sofa in my therapist's office. It was a sunny afternoon, but the shades were drawn to afford clients the sensation of privacy. I warmed my hands beneath my tightly crossed legs. I felt small and out of place, but I knew I was where I had to be.

"Where do you let your thoughts take you when you think of sex?" My therapist sat upright across from me, holding a cup of tea in her lap. I looked down at my own lap.

"Well, I don't really think about sex. I mean, only the fact that I 'should' have it, since I'm in a relationship and all."

She smiled and nodded, her lips slightly parting as though demonstrating for me how I might open my mouth and say more. When I didn't continue, she said, "I'm going to suggest that you allow yourself to engage in a sexual fantasy before we meet next. Try not to make judgments about what comes up—just notice where your mind takes you."

I cringed. *It won't take me very far.* My inner cynic launched forward by default, but I told Ms. Johnson that I would try. I was twenty-seven years old and tired of evading physical advances and questions about my sexual preferences from my partner. He'd even taken to leaving erotica around the apartment for me to read for inspiration. Yes, I would boldly go where I dared not go before. I would engage in a sexual fantasy and raise my therapist one by *sharing* it with my partner, I quickly decided.

Although this had been only my second therapy session, I had an unshared goal of being a scholar in my therapist's eyes—the case she would later describe in awe: "Rebecca was that rare and exceptional client whose personal advancement quickly superseded the need for therapy." The motivating factor behind my determination to rapidly move beyond therapy stemmed mostly from my deep-seated desire for overachievement. I was also afraid of what extensive therapy might demand of my bank account.

At home that night, I seized on a lull in conversation to explore this new me with my partner, Sam, while seated at the dinner table.

"So, I had this sexual fantasy earlier today," I began in between bites of salad.

"Mmm. Really? Tell me about it." Sam leaned in, gazing at me with desire and intrigue. He had been hungry for me to finally bring up this particular subject.

"Yeah, we were lying in bed, and you were on top of me. You raised my arms above my head…" I stopped.

"Uh-huh and *then* what?"

"Oh, that was all."

"Wait, what? That's it? That doesn't qualify as a sexual fantasy."

My shoulders slumped as my gaze fell down to my meal. I was disappointed in myself. I had hoped that once I began speaking, images and words might transcend my doubts and materialize into the sexy foreplay I had been unable to summon in my thoughts alone. But it still felt wrong to me. God or my parents or some other equally unwelcome guest had entered my mind, lurked in our kitchen, and shamed me.

While I couldn't seem to conjure in my mind's eye the stuff so many books and movies are made of, I had long dreamed of a more significant sexual fantasy. I ached to experience ecstasy—what I defined as the divine connection of mind, body, and spirit—in unity with a partner, but without shame or fear. However, I was terrified of sex. Talking about it, thinking about it, and God forbid, actually *doing* it. In fact, for the majority of my life, my God *did* forbid it, as did my parents, teachers, and seemingly all adults I held in high regard.

I grew up in the small city of La Crosse, Wisconsin, where I attended elementary school through college. Everyone who had known me as a child continued to think of me as the little girl I had once been. Now that I had left that town, I longed for an opportunity to create a new identity—one that didn't come attached to the labels shy, studious, and, as some of my peers saw me, sexually deprived.

My religion had taught me that sex before marriage was a sin, that masturbation was dirty, and that nudity was something to be embarrassed about. I attended a parochial school for the first half of my elementary school years, where I witnessed the church's hypocrisy—or at least the imperfection in its teachings. After the principal and his wife (my kindergarten teacher) were accused of child abuse, my parents moved my older brother and me over to the public school system. Though my interpretation of the institution of church remained foggy, I continued to believe the Bible to be the primary source of "right" and "wrong."

I had a strong, private relationship with God throughout my youth and young adulthood. I'd been taught to say my daily prayers, and the practice was one I continued into my adult years, beyond the point of parental expectation. It was a nightly ritual in which I found solace. I would habitually begin my prayers with, "Dear God, please let me have absolutely no nightmares and absolutely no bad dreams, and please forgive me for all the sins that I have done today." I didn't necessarily reflect on what these sins were—surely I'd committed *some*. I would then continue on to humbly ask for whatever it was my heart sought in the moment. My requests evolved from getting straight As to not being teased by my middle-school girlfriends to—by the time I reached high school—nearly begging to feel loved.

I'd always felt unconditional love from my family, but it wasn't enough for me—they were obligated to love me. I wanted to be looked at and held by someone unrelated to me in such a way that I'd be left with no doubt that I was worthy of love. That I was beautiful.

I felt anything but beautiful as a teenager. I hadn't yet learned how to tame my curly hair, and I'd inherited my father's oily skin, paving the way for severe acne by the time I reached fourteen. As a freshman in high school, I finally went to see a dermatologist. My mom went with me into the examination room. I sat on the edge of the exam table as the doctor closely explored my face. She spoke directly to my mom, as if I weren't my own person but merely a subject of study—a specimen on which the latest drugs could be tested.

"You can see how the condition has spread from across the forehead down the sides of the face to the jaw-line. The only surface that has been spared is the sensitive tissue around the eyes." She used a metal tool resembling a pen to point out the affected areas to my mom, who dutifully nodded along with great interest as she too closely inspected my face.

"What do you think can be done about it, Doctor?" my mom asked. I know that her intentions stemmed from love—she didn't like seeing her daughter suffer. But I felt like a disappointment. I was ashamed of my appearance, so I thought she must be too. I went home with several prescriptions, which helped to a degree, but ultimately the condition was one I would simply have to wait out through puberty. At least I was lucky that it was a temporary concern. If only future me could have told that to teenage me.

As for my hair, it wasn't until my senior year in high school that a friend of my mother's showed me how to embrace my curls and offered me her hair product in encouragement. What seemed like a small gesture made a significant impact on my confidence. Part of me resented the fact that my mother had never been one to French braid my hair or teach me a thing about fashion. It wasn't her forte, I would realize, but at the time it just seemed like she didn't think my looks were salvageable. I'd always hated sitting in the stylist's chair, the bright overhead lights accentuating my blemished skin that I was forced to look at in the massive mirror in front of me. With the help of her friend, however, going to get my hair cut became a bit more bearable.

I relied on God for comfort a lot during those days. His love was the conditional kind I sought, and I did feel loved by him. However, the downside of that kind of love was that I feared his judgment. Not only was he constantly watching my actions, he was listening to my thoughts. I had to keep them pure.

Though by the time I reached middle school my family no longer attended church, the public school system did a good job of making it clear what being "pure" entailed, especially when it came to sex. The sex ed curriculum emphasized the social, psychological, and health gains of practicing total abstinence and grossly exaggerated the dangers of sexual activity outside the context of marriage. By state law, contraceptive and safe-sex techniques were not to be discussed, except to warn of their risks and failures.

While in eighth grade, I witnessed the shame and the stigma applied to people who broke the rules. A girl who sat in front of me in study hall was becoming visibly rounder in the abdomen. Whispers of her potential pregnancy gave way to vocally charged accusations of immorality—and not just impurity but *dirtiness*. Fellow students were afraid to touch her, to talk to her. They simply stared and talked about her behind her back. She was well aware—that was painfully obvious. I felt sorry for her, but I dared not offer my support or I'd risk being made fun of too. I didn't want people to think I hung out with *that* kind of crowd.

Another girl, in my eighth-grade science class, got in trouble for passing a note. The teacher collected it and stood before the class as she read it silently to herself. Her jaw dropped, and her eyes widened as she stood in disbelief before declaring, "Megan, see me after class."

The room was rife with the glorified opportunity for gossip. It didn't take long for rumors to spread that the note had described a sexual encounter from the weekend before. And it became no secret that Megan was consequently required to attend counseling. Yes, sex was bad. I felt sorry for Megan—not just because of the unfair judgment she faced but because I liked her, and she seemed to be veering down a path of sin toward condemnation.

I didn't want either of these girls' lives for myself. I decided to avoid risk altogether and simply—so it seemed at the time—abstain from sex. It appeared the only sure way to guarantee I would not suffer from any of the following afflictions: parental disappointment and societal shame, impediment to my educational and career success due to unplanned pregnancy, slow and painful death after having become infected with AIDS or another sexually transmitted disease, and eternal damnation in hell. Having a long, healthy, and successful future and having a sex life seemed mutually exclusive, and I deemed the former the wiser of the two choices.

This belief foundation from my most formative years followed me even throughout college. I lived in the "dry" residence hall, where my peer group consisted of students with a more traditional religious background, so abstaining from sexual activity was commonplace. In some respect, it made my life easier, as moments of privacy in a shared dorm room were few and far between—and even then, the walls were paper thin and definite betrayers of "immoral" behavior. I was never asked out, anyway. I typically preferred to stay in the comfort of my dorm room, listening to music and writing in my journal, rather than attend social events.

Since sex with a partner was unobtainable, self-pleasure might have been a safe substitute for my body's natural sex drive. However, by my early adulthood, the temptation to touch myself in a sexual way was simply nonexistent. I didn't even allow my thoughts to entertain such a possibility. The whole concept seemed trivial—a mere distraction from my studies or even a decent novel.

I didn't always feel that way. I first experimented with masturbation around the age of eleven, though I didn't know what it was. I thought I had discovered a secret path to bliss that no one else knew about—and I didn't want to share it. It was the childhood kind of masturbation, fully clothed and completely quiet, beginning my habit of restraining my breath during anything sexual. It was always done in private, of course, because not only did I not want to share my secret but I thought that it was probably "wrong" to touch myself "down there." The only time my parents referred to my genital region was when it came time to bathe. My mom always reminded me to "wash my duty." It wasn't until I was well into my adult life that I learned *duty* wasn't really an official word for vagina. My thoughts during my early experiments were not of the sexual variety. Even if I'd connected what I was doing to sex, I was clothed and silent—so my brain was too.

Death drove my first experience with the act. I was in bed crying about my grandmother's recent passing, feeling bad that I hadn't made more of an effort to know her. I held myself between the legs; it was a warm and comforting position. As the pain became more wrenching, my body writhed with sobbing, and my hands moved my clothing in such a way that physically aroused me. I didn't know what was happening, but I kept crying and allowing the sensation to increase. Finally, I felt release, and my heart slowed from its frenzied state as my breathing began to calm. I felt soothed. I was finally able to sleep.

Though I enjoyed my secret self-pleasure sessions as a child, once I reached middle school and learned that it was called masturbation (and was not so secret after all), I refrained from the practice. I could tell by the tone my teacher used when she talked about it that it was dirty. I now knew it was a sexual act and, therefore, was definitely wrong for me to enjoy.

Also while in middle school, I experienced my first period. I had dreaded its arrival because it would mean I'd have to talk about my body with my mom. She had already started teasingly calling me "Little Boobies," to my mortification. I'd have preferred to hide the fact that my body was changing.

"We're going to have to go bra shopping for you," my mom said one day. Her tone demonstrated excitement for the fact that her daughter was becoming a woman. I could feel her longing to celebrate this rite of passage with her only daughter. She made a distinction between becoming a young woman and becoming a sexual being, but I did not. I so deeply wanted to deny both parts of me. There was something shameful in what was happening to my body—I knew it, because my dad left the room anytime my mom brought it up.

"Mom! Winter is coming, and winter means *sweaters*." The last word rang with the critical disgust of teenage rebellion. How funny that my rebellion was against grown-up things when most teens wanted more of those. I wanted to move on from the topic as quickly as possible and retreat to my bedroom to put on multiple layers of clothing to cover the two offending parties.

"Little boobies, ha-ha!" I could hear my brother snickering from the next room on my way up the stairs.

As much as I feared my mother's enthusiastic reaction to my period, a greater fear was that it would come while I was at school. I was sure the blood would leak through my pants for everyone to see, thereby making me an urban legend of my middle school—if not the entire state of Wisconsin. Horrible stories had circulated among my female friends of similar situations happening to fellow classmates. Whether they were true or idle gossip, no one knew for sure.

My period ended up coming on a weekend when I was fourteen, to my great relief. After flushing the evidence down the toilet (or so I thought), I slowly made my way downstairs to the kitchen, where I warily told my mom what had happened. She was indeed excited, but thankfully did not overreact. That position, however, was readily employed by my brother.

"Ohmigod! There is *blood* in the toilet!" My whole family heard him yell from the top of the stairs. You'd think he'd discovered a dead body.

"Gross!" The shouting continued.

My mom looked at me with sympathetic eyes. "Enough, Matt!"

My insides coiled, but I maintained a silent reserve. I was too humiliated to defend myself. I waited for my brother to retreat to his room before withdrawing to my own room, defeated.

I dreaded the return of this monthly experiment with torture. That dread manifested into something very real: I did not get a single period for the next two years.

I was relieved to not have to deal with a monthly cycle and the accompanying reminder of my sexuality, but I knew it must mean something was wrong with me. Eventually my family doctor confirmed that assumption when I went in for my annual sports physical. The gymnastics season was about to start. I'd wanted so badly to be one of those strong, self-confident girls whose Olympic careers I'd followed with zeal since elementary school. My favorite event was the floor routine. I aspired to express my creativity, strength, and grace in response to music. I envisioned myself actually feeling pretty in the competition leotards; I thought their sparkle and shine might make up for the uncomfortable skin I wore underneath. As it turned out, I ended up dreading competitions; rather than feel pretty, I felt publicly displayed. I endured the discomfort for two full seasons, but not before getting through the physical exam.

"You're menstruating regularly now, right?" the doctor asked as a matter of custom, with the tone that it was an unnecessary question to ask someone at the ripe old age of sixteen.

I felt my face flush as I admitted, "Well…no." I told her I had gotten my period only once, two years before.

"What?" she exclaimed, dropping her pen. "We have to get you on birth control right away! You could get osteoporosis!"

Osteo-what?! Whatever that was, it sounded bad. I marveled at the realization that to have a regular period meant risking getting pregnant, and to not have a regular period meant risking some horrible disease. Everything related to sexuality was dangerous.

She continued to tell me that if I ever wanted to have kids, it might be difficult for me to get pregnant, but technology was evolving, and there might be help for my "condition," never really explaining what that condition was. My mind interpreted her words as reinforcement that there was something inherently wrong with me, with my femininity and my sexuality.

I was put on birth control and would remain on it for ten years. Sleepovers with friends or overnight gymnastics meets now required strategic planning. I would sneak into the bathroom with my pill pack to take the prescribed daily dose. I couldn't let anyone know I was on birth control. Not only might they know there was something wrong with my body, but they might also think I was sexually active, and *that* would mean I was definitely going to hell.

In the end, my secrets were uncovered. Teenage girls should be international spies. Before bed during one sleepover, I didn't try to hide the location of my journal. I trusted the one other person there, one of my closest friends. I pulled it out from between my mattress and box spring and wrote a few reflections before placing it back in position and going to sleep. The following morning, the lock that had recently been installed on my bedroom door to keep my brother out was used against me. I stepped out to go to the bathroom, and when I returned, I found that my friend had locked herself inside my room. At first I thought she was simply being playful. My initial laughter gave way to nervous anxiety, followed by panic when I heard the sound of pages turning. She'd retrieved my journal and was leisurely settling in for a good read.

"Sara, let me in." I pounded on the door. "This isn't funny!"

I could hear her snickering. Tears laced my eyes. I knew I'd never forget that moment. I feared that my faith in friendship would be forever tainted by this one broken bond.

When she finally opened the door with a smile on her face, as if nothing had happened, I understood the following days at school would be hell. She told all the girls in my circle of friends everything: my current crush, the shame I felt about my skin, my being on birth control, and my fear of never being loved. She'd told me some of her secrets, but I kept myself from retaliating with them. I instead just stopped hanging out with her—and several of the other friends in the group. I began to turn from investing in social relationships to cultivating a deeper relationship with myself.

I escaped inside my own private world by listening to music, writing, and talking to God. I favored gospel music at the time—namely early albums by Aretha Franklin and Whitney Houston. I harbored a secret fantasy to be a Southern black woman. Not only did I revel in the vocal expression of their souls that seemed intrinsically unique to their culture, but I felt being a black person would offer me a socially accepted opportunity to fight against oppression. I wanted a justifiable reason to be seen as a victim. I felt oppressed in my own little, middle-class, whitegirl world, but I did not feel worthy of compassion and consolation from others; I hadn't suffered enough.

If I could not be black, I at least wanted to be Jewish. My writing at the time consisted predominantly of short stories told by young Jewish girls escaping Nazi persecution. I was obsessed with this era in history—the epitome of worthy victimhood. I felt such profound compassion for what Holocaust victims had gone through that part of me yearned to be one of them myself. While other girls my age were dreaming of vacations in Florida or California, my prevailing travel aspiration was to visit the Holocaust Memorial Museum in Washington, DC. I wanted to see the artifacts with my own eyes, to sink into their owners' stories and their suffering and feel *one* with them. Reliving their pain would make me feel alive.

I composed various journal entries to God. Mostly I asked questions regarding entry into heaven or hell. I came up with imaginative scenarios where acts that were labeled a sin in the Bible might be dually considered circumstances of defense and innocence. What of the parent who murdered someone who was about to attack her child? And what about the child who hadn't yet learned what was "right" and "wrong" when he died? I just couldn't grasp how eternal happiness or suffering after death could be determined by absolute standards. Nonetheless, I didn't want to take any chances by violating rules myself, especially the ones such as sex before marriage for which I could not think of good exceptions.

The rules I applied to myself, I didn't think necessarily applied to others. My brother, for example, was allowed to date and be alone with his girlfriend in his bedroom. I had once even uncovered a duffel bag of porn magazines in his closet, to which my mom simply said, "I'll let your father decide how he wants to handle that." Dad discreetly shrugged it off with the reply, "Boys will be boys." Several of my friends had been in committed relationships throughout high school and college, were sexually active, and had established sex-positive attitudes.

I, on the other hand, felt like an outcast in the realm of sex and relationships. Sex intimidated me. All of the messages I'd received in school—the threat of STDs, teenage pregnancy and, worst of all, the shame of having premarital sex—was enough to make me want to lock myself in a cave where no one could ever penetrate me, screaming like Eliza Doolittle, "I'm a good girl, I am!"

During the spring before my final semester of college, one of my sex-positive friends introduced me to the idea of using sex toys. We had been sitting at a quiet café in downtown La Crosse when I whispered I had never used a sexual aid.

"*What*? You've never used a dildo…or a vibrator…or *anything*?" she exclaimed.

I sank into our booth, shielding my face with my hands.

My friend took no note of my discomfort, however, and generously offered, "That's it! I am going shopping for you!" I was about to leave for a summer job in Colorado, and she insisted she was going to mail a box full of "goodies" to my place of employment. I begged her to have mercy and not follow through with that idea. The staff accommodations would consist of one large room with twenty bunk beds—I could predict my future should such a package arrive, and it involved an exorbitant amount of teasing and the end of my blissful summer job. She finally agreed not to send the package.

I was ashamed to have sex yet ashamed not to. I thought I was the only twenty-two-year-old virgin in my town—and perhaps the world. I hadn't even been in a relationship. Sure, I'd been kissed a few times, but that was it. I tried to comfort myself with the words of some of the men I'd been interested in: "You're the kind of girl a man marries, not one that he just dates." I figured I was supposed to be flattered—and part of me was. In private, however, I entertained a truly dark desire: to be taken advantage of. No, *really* taken advantage of. I wanted to be raped. I could finally lose my shameful virginity, yet still go to heaven because *I* had done nothing wrong. The scenario would serve another purpose—it would also make me a victim. I'd finally be worthy of comfort, of love.

Almost immediately after college graduation, I departed for Nashville, Tennessee, where I hoped to fuel my passion for live music. Though I'd excelled in my coursework, I considered my real college education to have come from my leadership role in bringing live music to campus. I took great pride in bringing an event from concept to fruition, making connections with booking agents, tour managers, and musical artists themselves in the process. Standing in the back of a venue on event night was magical. I could feel the excitement and energy circulating among the audience in anticipation of the band's arrival while I reflected on the activity board's hard work. *We did this. We brought joy to these people's lives tonight.* I felt such a rush from providing opportunities for others to experience the deep gratification that music brought to my own soul. I experienced concerts as a reprieve from the monotony and occasional pain of everyday life.

I used the connections I established in college to obtain employment with a booking agency shortly after my arrival in Music City USA. I supplemented my income with a part-time position at the Ryman Auditorium—an internationally renowned music venue that was once the home of the Grand Ole Opry. However, after one year working in the music business, I became disheartened by the bureaucracy. My soul sought deeper fulfillment. I maintained my evening position at the Ryman Auditorium while I spent the next two years working full-time for Big Brothers Big Sisters. Though I loved the service the organization provided for at-risk youth, I still felt empty. Work of any kind was not my answer. I wanted a partner in life. I wanted to feel loved.

I had the first relationship of my life early in my first year in Nashville. It only lasted six months, but his overpowering energy attached itself to me for years. At first I basked in the glow of being pursued by a man. He hunted me with remarkable persistence. He called me repeatedly throughout each day; it took great effort on my part to carry through with a farewell. Though I recognized that the frequency and duration of his phone calls could have been seen as red flags, I was flattered that someone felt compelled to show me that level of devotion.

When Ryan and I established ourselves as a couple, I felt such relief that I was finally someone's girlfriend. But I realized that label came with expectations. Initially, he appeared very patient and respectful of my sexual inhibitions and told me he was in no rush. I felt so blessed to have found someone so willing to wait until I was ready. But his early veneration gave way to contempt before long.

"I always end up with virgins." He smirked. "I'm so tired of this."

I surrendered to his physical advances a month into our relationship. I was twenty-four years old and I figured that even God would approve at this point. People had babies at age twenty-four. I wasn't looking to get pregnant, but maybe just being at procreation age was enough to render the act acceptable in God's eyes, or so I tried to convince myself.

Ryan and I had been sitting on the living room couch, paging through an atlas of photos taken of the earth from space and cities taken from airplanes high above. We both loved geography; we wanted to understand our own place in this giant universe and perhaps make sense of the purpose of it all. When we finished going through the book and the animated air in the room gave way to silence, he gazed intensely into my eyes, picked me up, and brought me to the bedroom. I knew this was it. I clung to the fact that I had felt connected to him while leafing through the picture book, sharing our dreams of world travel. I prayed that connection would transfer to the physical realm, so that my body might intuitively know how to respond to his.

He gently stroked my body, my inner thighs, my stomach, and subsequently reached down to the folds and crevices between my legs. He moistened and massaged my clitoris. *I am actually turned on,* I thought with surprise. I was amazed he knew exactly where to go—for I had hardly known myself. But then he removed his own pants and attempted to penetrate me.

"Oww!" I quietly exclaimed. I had expected it to hurt, so I was exceedingly sensitive to the stretch of my vaginal muscles. He pulled back to attempt to reenter more slowly.

"Ahhh, that hurts!" I repeated.

He sighed in exasperation. "Rebecca, it has to go in sometime. It won't hurt once I get past your hymen. You've got to let me just break through it."

We were too far along now, I agreed. I let him infiltrate me as I softly cried. It wasn't long before he came. We cleaned up his semen and my blood and that was it. Where was the pleasure? He promised it would come after the first time. He went right to sleep, but I lay awake for quite some time. All those years of anticipation and lecture on the sacredness of this first time. It didn't feel so sacred. I had sex so that I would finally feel like the woman I believed my age signified. But I still didn't feel like a woman. I didn't enjoy it, so instead I felt damaged. *Did I make a mistake?* I thought. But maybe he was right; the next time would be better.

It never got better. I dreaded each sexual encounter with the anxiety I had experienced before an important exam. I did feel I was being tested. My sexuality was put on trial. If I didn't enjoy his advances, or pretend like I had, I was met with his scorn. He looked at me like...there was something wrong with me. I'd been discovered. My doctor's reaction from years before was reaffirmed.

Beyond that, our relationship tested my individuality. Ryan wanted to see me every night after work, even when I was exhausted or had other interests I ached to pursue. His demands chipped away at my identity, and I left pieces of me in his musky old apartment each time I guiltily consented to his phone call demanding I come over. I would have preferred to go out dancing. My high school gymnastics classes had given me rhythm, and in a brave moment in college, I signed up for a swing and social dance class. I soon realized dancing was an opportunity to experience intimacy without sex. I could remain fully clothed, in public, and I could be touched without immediately recoiling, as I'd become accustomed to doing while wearing my protective "no sex here" shield. In Nashville, the abundance of opportunities to dance inspired me to dance more. I began attending lindy exchanges, rather like a dance conference, where dancers from all over the region—and sometimes the world—took lindy hop classes and participated in evening dances that often extended until sunrise. I had less and less time for dancing because of Ryan's demands on my time.

I felt good after sex with Ryan only once, and it was with a perverse pleasure that had nothing to do with a boyfriend or love or, certainly, my own self-worth. I was still on the birth control pill to regulate my cycle, so Ryan felt it wasn't necessary to use condoms. Then one morning I realized with panic that I'd forgotten to take the pill the night before. When I told him, he paced across his apartment in a fit of rage.

"What? You forgot to take your pill? I can't believe you forgot! Ohmigod, Rebecca..."

"Wait, you're the one that never wants to use a condom! Why is protection solely *my* responsibility?"

He stopped yelling. He knew I was right. I was angry with him and scared about our mistake, but part of me felt like a character in a soap opera, which actually made me feel somewhat proud. I was arguing about sex. I was *having* sex. Finally. At least I could now fit in with my peers.

I knew it was an unhealthy relationship. I tried to end it several times over the course of our six months together, but every time I would start to state my decision, he would interject:

"You're not breaking up with me, are you? You can't do that. I love you."

"Why do you love me, Ryan?" I'd ask. I didn't feel loved.

"Because you're beautiful. And you're nice to me."

That's it? That's what love is?

Maybe I had it wrong. Maybe I just didn't know how simple love really was. It did hurt me to see him cry, after all. I thought I needed to demonstrate love to another in order to be lovable to myself. I didn't know any better. I was well educated in the realm of books and standardized tests, but I knew nothing about love and the value of self.

"I love you too," I'd reply. I wanted to try the words on. Perhaps if I spoke them out loud, I'd know if they rang true for me or not. I still wasn't sure.

"Thank you." He held me tightly in desperation. We were still a couple.

After a visit home to Wisconsin, however, away from his overwhelming energy, I realized how relieved I felt to be away from him. I agreed to meet him during my lunch hour on my first day back in Nashville. He approached me in the parking lot outside the café and embraced me. I let him hold me as I stared off into the distance with empty eyes.

"I missed you." He sighed with deep emotion. I said nothing.

We entered the café, and as we stood in line for a seat, he stood back and lifted my face. "You didn't say that you missed me."

Here was my moment. I looked him in the eye and replied, "No, I didn't."

He began to cry. I held my ground. We didn't make it to a table to have lunch. He drove home. But he called me later that night, crying and begging that I still remain his friend.

"I need you, Rebecca. You're my only friend. What will I do without you?"

What kind of person can I be if I deny him even a friendship? I thought. And so our relationship went on. We weren't a couple, but everyone thought that we were. I owed him nothing, but he thought I owed him my most intrinsic gift. I continued to allow myself to be subject to his needs and responsible for his happiness. His taunts continued and progressed.

"What kind of a friend are you, if you see me suffering from not having my sexual needs met and don't do anything about it?" His words were like daggers to both my heart and my self-esteem. I knew in my head they were twisted and sick, but I lacked the courage to walk away. I didn't want to hurt him, so I instead hurt myself. I thought that by saying no to sex I must not be an adult, a woman. All adults wanted sex, right? And I wanted so desperately to be a woman.

I cringed every time he approached me, desire burning in his eyes, extending his hand for me to take so he could lead me to the bedroom. I came to loathe that room—the blankets, the mismatched sheets, the smell of his sex. I lay there, going through the motions. I allowed my mouth to be forced open by his penis. I had no voice.

I had to escape. Not just emotionally—that wasn't enough—but physically, geographically too. All my life I'd dreamed of faraway places, places in which I thought I could avoid my anxiety around boys, reinvent myself. Those fantasies had encouraged me to study abroad during college, so I knew what good travel could do. They'd even gotten me out of La Crosse, finally—even temporarily. But I credit my background in dancing with what little courage and self-confidence I finally mustered now, to get me out of Nashville. I knew I had grace. I had once kept my own schedule, untied to another's demands.

I picked Argentina—the farthest inhabited country south—as my country of escape, and plotted my departure for six months later. But even before departing on my international adventure, my world began to change when I moved out of an apartment I'd shared with two women, and into a house with three male lindy hop dancers—one of whom was my dance teacher, Micah.

Micah and I developed an intimate rapport during my final six months in Nashville. We even took a road trip to New Orleans, staying with a friend of his, during which we crossed the line away from just friends while indulging in hurricane drinks on Bourbon Street. Dancing on the bar's balcony, we broke the "touch barrier." When I leaned in for a hug, we progressed to a full-on make-out session well beyond any duration I had ever experienced. It likely would have continued even longer, had we not been interrupted by an admiring man at the other end of the bar.

"Excuse me, but I've been watching you two make out for the last, oh"—he glanced at his watch—"hour and fifteen minutes, and I've just got to say *wow*! Way to go!"

I was impressed, too. Not just at our commitment to the cause at hand, but at the fact that Micah had wanted to kiss me. He was highly sought after in the dance scene. I'd never felt pretty enough for him. The shift in our dynamic did not cause us to consider developing a committed relationship—I knew I would not be returning to Nashville after my travel adventure. But we allowed our new physical connection to extend throughout the New Orleans trip. The second twin bed in his friend's spare bedroom experienced no use after the first night—but we did not have sex.

At the time he too was God-fearing, and though Micah's lifestyle blurred the biblical lines more than mine did, he did not want to "damage" me any further than our encounters already had. I was not seeking sex, anyway. I was craving the feeling of being worthy of being someone's sexual partner. If we articulated it wasn't anything about me, that it was God who kept us from having sex, I could relax into the beauty of simply feeling desired.

I reveled in what we shared. I would lie with him and ponder with gratitude, *I get to be his girl for tonight.* I knew it wouldn't be likely to have him alone like this once we returned to Nashville. Our house was a landing post for not only the four of us roommates but a plethora of local and out-of-town dancers on any given night. We did try, however. He would discreetly sneak up to my second-floor bedroom or I down to his basement unit. We wanted to keep our nighttime sessions private. We both felt guilty about the nature of our relationship. My departure from Nashville was an awkward one, in that regard—things felt messy and unresolved. He feared he was corrupting my purity—leading me down the path of casual foreplay he was trying to no longer choose for himself. I sensed that he also was afraid I would become attached to something he wasn't capable of giving me—a sense of belonging.

I, on the other hand, felt I was selfishly tempting him away from his preferred state of being. But the relationship did offer me something very important—a lesson in self-worth. Many a night, Micah would hold me and repeatedly assure me that I deserved better than what Ryan had offered me. Not only did I gain a new level of comfort with simply being held, but I began to believe in my own value as an individual.

I took that message with me as I left for Argentina—where the first day of my transformative journey began.

2
A Brazilian in Buenos Aires

WITH NO MORE than a casual goodbye on the phone to Ryan and a long hug goodbye to Micah, I loaded my car with all of my personal possessions and embarked on the 750-mile journey from my home in Nashville to my parents' home in La Crosse. I would drop my belongings at their house before embarking on a six-week adventure, traveling independently throughout Argentina. Upon my return, I would reload my car and drive another 2,000 miles to where I would create a new home for myself in Portland, Oregon. I had been diligently saving money over the last several months, and I figured I had just enough in savings to last until my arrival in Portland, where I hoped to find a meaningful job as quickly as possible.

I knew no one in Portland, which was exactly what I craved. I was also inspired by the proximity to the ocean and the mountains and the progressive culture that seemed to mesh more with the direction my heart was leading me. I'd heard that Portland had a thriving bike culture, an abundance of vegan food, and outdoor adventure. It sounded nothing like La Crosse, nothing like Nashville. I wanted in.

But Argentina would come first. I occasionally feared what challenges might confront me while traveling alone in a country and culture I knew next to nothing about, but I didn't care. I simply knew I had to go. I flew into Mendoza, Argentina, and toured Patagonia by bus before landing in Buenos Aires. As always, my journal served as my best confidant.

> *After two weeks traveling independently in the Andean region of Argentina, I am now finally on the bus to the city I have read so much about—Buenos Aires. I would like to take this opportunity to write about some realizations I had yesterday. Not only am I on this trip alone, I actually have no friends or home to return to. Usually when people have been traveling for a while, they eventually crave going "home" to the place and environment they are familiar with, have a routine at, where their belongings are, and where their friends and family reside. I guess I have had occasional cravings for "home," though "home" to me is the United States—where my language is spoken and I understand the culture. I have no more than that to return to.*
>
> *My current "friends" are so fleeting. Everyone whose path I've crossed while on this trip I know I will most likely never see again. For one or two days, my life and source of social interaction depends on a particular person or group of people. I can call them or go to where they're staying, but [then] that number is no longer valid. They've touched my past, but are no longer a part of my present or future. In time, I will forget their names, and may even forget we ever met. It is possible that on occasion I may meet someone I really connect with—someone that will somehow affect my future, but it hasn't happened yet.*

I ARRIVED AT the 06 Central Hostel in downtown Buenos Aires and checked into a dorm room with six beds. I said a silent prayer for quiet roommates—the fewer, the better. I lucked out and got only two: a tall, awkward Italian man named Marco, who spoke not a word of English (or anything but Italian), and a Brazilian man named Boris. Ponytailed with a double-pierced ear, he was, to me, exotic and attractive but unattainable. Chances were a language barrier would keep us from communicating in any meaningful way.

That first night I sat at a long table in the common area with my laptop, likely journaling about the artisan chocolate I'd indulged in while in Bariloche. I was content to be alone at the corner of the table, as it meant no one had to know I did not speak Spanish (despite my best efforts in a beginner class I took before leaving Nashville). I feared being considered what I believed I was—an ignorant American. And then Boris, sitting at the opposite end of the table, said something to me. Instead of being put off by my bewildered look, he simply switched to English.

Damn. Busted. I replied—and he spoke again. Despite my intentions, I was having a conversation. And despite myself, I was pleased to have someone with whom I could talk for a bit. He worked for an American company and was fluent in English. Our conversation evolved from the standard, "Where are you from? How long are you here?" to our shared passion for blues music. I told him that I was a lindy hop and blues dancer.

"I'm familiar with lindy hop dancing but *blues* dancing? What is that?" he asked.

"Blues dancing is also a contemporary partner dance with African roots, but it's led by the music, rather than specific dance steps. To me, it's more liberating than lindy hop, because of its freedom from rules and restrictions. It's a dance strongly connected to emotion, ranging from extreme joy to extreme sadness. I love it so much because it gets me out of my head—you *have* to be out of your head and into your body to dance, which is normally somewhere I don't want to be," I released a shy giggle. I could see he was intrigued, so I continued.

"It's actually helped me get over the fear of being touched—when you blues dance, you actually get to be held. Dancing to the blues feels like a big, beautiful hug. It's a relationship free of expectation, since it only has to last until the song ends."

I surprised myself by sharing the personal details of my experience with Boris.

"Wow, it sounds beautiful. I'd love to see what it looks like."

Encouraged by his positive reaction, I moved to sit next to him so that I could show him some videos of the dance on my computer. When I was done, he extended the time we sat next to each other by showing me shaky footage of the punk rock band he played drums in. As the evening progressed, he shared that he was ending an intense ten-year relationship. His time in Buenos Aires was meant to clear his head. I divulged that I also was escaping an unhealthy relationship.

When, tired, we moved our things into the dorm room, we found Marco already in bed, but Boris and I were having a hard time ending our conversation. I lay on my bottom bunk, and he sat down on the floor beside me with his arms wrapped tightly around his bent knees, leaning against the wall by the head of my bed. Every time a lull in the conversation would suggest impending sleep, one of us would seize the opportunity to fill it.

"One of my best friends moved away to England. He's studying at Oxford. I haven't told him this, but I really miss him," Boris said once.

I reopened my eyes and noticed the glimmer of relief in his own: I was still awake. He continued, "I really admire his courage for moving abroad. I want to leave Brazil too. Fuck Brazil. I want to see the world. There's so much more out there."

"So what is stopping you?"

"My friends in Brazil say I'd be crazy to leave my job. Everyone wants to work for this company, and if I left I'd have to start all over. There would be no guarantee I could get a job like this again." As Boris shared his dream, the hunger in his eyes was reflective of my own longing for something more.

Though I didn't want the night to end, I regretfully expressed that exhaustion had taken over my body. With a hint of disappointment, but in a nurturing tone of acceptance, Boris wished me a good night and retreated to his top bunk on the opposite side of the room. I lay awake for a while, smiling about my new friend. I had a strong suspicion he was beginning to see me in more than just a friendly way. I started plotting how to block any advances. My fear and shame around sex were so deeply embedded in my brain they kept me from wanting to open myself to any relationship beyond friendship. My biggest wall was Boris's own: he'd be returning to Brazil in four days anyway. How much could happen?

THE NEXT TWO days began with what became my weekday routine in Buenos Aires. My alarm would go off at 10:55 a.m., which gave me five minutes to take advantage of the hostel's free breakfast. I would gather my *dos medialunas con mermelada de durazno* ("two croissants with peach jam") and *jugo de naranja* ("orange juice") and leisurely dine at the communal table on the patio. For those two days, I had had the special treat that Boris would already be there telecommuting. I delighted in his morning company before I had to get ready to attend my Spanish lesson, followed by a tango lesson later in the afternoon.

In the evenings Boris and I would team up to do a bit of sightseeing. That first night on the town, Thursday, he invited me to join Marco and him for dinner at a pizzeria down the street. I had already eaten, but I eagerly joined them to continue exploring this compelling Brazilian man. Doing so with Marco present made me feel safe. Seated at the dinner table, Boris pulled from the cavities of his brain the few Italian words he remembered from school so that we could interact somewhat within our trio. Marco invited Boris and me to join him for a concert after dinner, but we took turns saying we preferred to stay in for the night. It wasn't yet spoken, but we both felt a seed of promise at the opportunity to be alone together.

Relaxing on the patio back at the hostel, we stole penetrating glances at each other in between bashful withdrawals of focused attention. Conversation came naturally, but our thoughts playfully considered a connection beyond merely verbal territory.

"Do you want to do something together tonight?" Boris asked with the same look of hopeful yearning I had recognized the night before.

"What did you have in mind?" My heart began to race.

"Do you like wine? I can buy a bottle, and we can share it back here."

"That sounds great." I released a sigh of appreciation that my nerves would soon be able to experience a respite.

He went out to buy a bottle and returned shortly to where I'd continued to sit on the patio.

"Ready?" he asked.

"Sure!" I said enthusiastically, while remaining seated at the communal table.

Boris moved to step inside our dorm room.

"Oh," I said with surprise. "You mean in there?"

"Yes, of course," he answered curiously.

My insecurities began to boil. I had already demonstrated the innocence of a child, not the confidence of an adult woman, by expressing surprise that he had intended us to share the wine privately. Hesitantly, I followed him into the room. My mind fought flashbacks of being led to another bedroom in my past, but I knew this was a different man. This was one who sparked emotions in me that I had never felt with anyone else, even though I still did not know him well.

Relax, Rebecca, I thought. *Sharing wine with a man in a hostel bedroom does not mean it will lead to sex.* My intuition, however, told me two things: one, that he was a good man, nothing like Ryan back in Nashville and, two, that it likely would lead to sex—if not now, then soon.

Boris locked the door behind us. I was acutely aware of this extra step—a certain sign that something private was about to happen. I was somewhat scared to be there, but I wanted to take this next step nonetheless. We opened the bottle of wine and began listening to music on my laptop. B. B. King's "The Thrill Is Gone" joined the rotation. The sheer beauty of the opening notes evoked feelings of foreplay in my mind, and I could tell that Boris was particularly moved as well.

King's voice eased into a seductive moan as I stood to allow the music to pass through my body. I was inspired to express the intensity of what I was experiencing, and I invited Boris to dance with me.

Our eyes met as we swayed in a close embrace and quietly sang along to the words that transcended continents, languages, and cultures to land in the hearts and memories of both our beings.

I led Boris through some basic blues moves, isolating and rolling various parts of my body to accentuate and hit particular notes, pausing to breathe slower and deeper in communion with the more profound parts of the song. The dance allowed me the freedom to express myself without feeling vulnerable. Much as dancing is an excellent outlet for the socially awkward because it doesn't require talking, it is equally an effective outlet for the sexually inhibited because it doesn't require nudity. I just needed to respond instinctually to the music. It felt like I was coming home to myself. I let go of my inhibitions a little more as the song began to come to a close.

Although the lyrics suggest a triumphant release of attachment, our experience was contradictory. We were falling under each other's spell. One more pass around the room, and Boris pressed me up against the wall of lockers and kissed me passionately. I'd never been kissed like that. This was a *Latin* kiss. I found myself wondering if the term *French kiss* should be revised.

We were hooked—"just friends" be gone. The fairy godmother sprinkled her magic stardust, and we were magnetically connected from that point on. Until Sunday, that is. Three days away.

The night ended sweetly. We kissed some more, and then some more, before retreating to our respective bunks for the night. So far, so good. I wasn't completely found out yet. *I might still be a woman in his eyes,* I considered.

FRIDAY NIGHT WE met up after our daily activities and joined two other couples I had met through my tango dance class for dinner and salsa dancing. At dinner, Boris's and my hands joined under the table, and at the dance our eyes continuously sought connection. When I danced with another man from our group, Boris openly demonstrated his jealousy. I took pleasure in the fact that he saw me as desirable enough to catch the eye of this attractive other man and felt okay with that feeling because I wasn't playing with Boris; this other man was not a threat to him. I was, instead, enthralled with this striking Brazilian man who felt so familiar to me.

We closed the night in true *porteño* style, the way Buenos Aires natives do, not returning to the hostel until 5:00 a.m. Boris and I were disappointed to find new roommates in our dorm, but our sheer exhaustion would have prevented any degree of intimacy anyway. We went straight to our respective beds.

Saturday would be the first—and only—full day that Boris and I would spend together in Buenos Aires. We took full advantage of it, walking along the newly developed waterfront of Puerto Madero before crossing the river and renting bikes to explore Costanera Sur, an ecological reserve of trails amid gorgeous marsh and grassland. It was a refreshing place to escape the noise of the city and find some privacy, but the severity of the mosquitos prevented us from indulging too long.

The geography of Costanera Sur reminded me of La Crosse. I had traversed trails like this by bike many times throughout my life, as they weaved behind both my elementary school and my college campus. I found rare moments of seclusion on those trails, away from my family and, later, away from my roommates. I finally had a place to just be. I filled journal after journal while sitting on benches among the wetlands; I wrote poetry depicting both the beauty of nature and the anguish of my adolescent soul. Always, I daydreamed of faraway places.

And now here I was, nearly six thousand miles south, and my surroundings looked the same as where I'd come from. A deeper look, of course, revealed that I couldn't have been farther away—Buenos Aires flora could not survive in La Crosse. I was different too. The distance from home had changed me. I had a companion by my side, an exotic man with whom I'd already become quite comfortable. How could a man from so far away—raised with a different culture, language, and religion—have so much in common with me? Why did he feel so familiar?

I left the questions to hang within me. I knew I was inexperienced in the realm of love. *I'll likely feel this way with many men in my future,* I mused. *This particular story has an obvious and impending ending. A few more days, and our relationship will simply become fodder for nostalgia.*

But there would be time to contemplate the future later. All I knew was that now, our experience together at what we dubbed Puerto Mosquito was blissful. My heart fluttered with each stroke of Boris's touch. I delighted in visibly being part of a couple. When you're painfully single, couples in love can be spotted around every corner—or at least couples in lust. For once, I was one of them. To experiment with the idea of being in a romantic partnership while in public felt safe to me. There was no pressure to go too far.

Later, back in our room, we wondered how we should end the night. It was St. Patrick's Day—a good opportunity to celebrate. It was also Boris's last night in Buenos Aires before returning to Brazil. I sat on my bed as he sat cross-legged on the floor in front of me.

"I just had a crazy idea," he began. "I really don't want to spend my last night with you in this dorm room. Would you be open to me getting us a hotel room?"

I felt an intense wave of inner conflict. I was simultaneously flattered, excited, and terrified. Our mere four days together had come to this. My instinct told me that this next step was one I should take, and I interpreted that message as approval from God. So, I knew that if I said no, it would be strictly out of fear and my own insecurities. I was on this trip to stretch my boundaries, to challenge myself and see what came up for me. I knew what I needed to do.

"I'll agree…on two conditions. One, we get ice cream first and, two, we get a bottle of wine for the room." The little girl in me was craving the comfort of a sweet and familiar physical sensation, and the emerging woman was inviting me to experiment with new aspects of pleasure.

I thought Boris was going to jump for joy, as I could feel his energy level heighten, but he remained seated, allowing only a generous smile to grace his face.

"Great," he said quietly, with the adorable accent that touched my heart.

I walked cautiously with him to an ice cream shop. My stomach was a bundle of nerves. I trusted my desire to share this night with him, but I also felt like each step was bringing me closer to impending doom. *Well, I'll probably never see him again after tomorrow. Once he realizes I have no idea what I'm doing in bed, it will just be a matter of passing a few more hours with him. At least I won't regret not trying.*

We ate our ice cream and continued our walk to find a liquor store. It was too late to purchase a bottle from a wine shop, so Boris came up with the idea of buying a bottle from a restaurant. The manager on duty eyed us suspiciously, contemplating if he should sell us a bottle without our having been patrons at his establishment. Boris managed to charm him with a gesture toward me and a plea along the lines of "Please be a gentleman—it's for the *lady*." He finally acquiesced and, bottle in hand, we found the nearest decent-looking hotel to check in to for the night.

We approached the front desk carrying a bottle of wine and no luggage. I wondered how many times the hotel staff had seen this scenario. I had been informed by locals that Buenos Aires was infamous for its *albergues transitorios,* hotel rooms rentable by the hour for young couples needing a reprieve from their parents or married individuals needing a reprieve from their spouses. But this was not a hotel of that sort—the entrance was not hidden by protective walls, and the edifice lacked decorative neon lights.

We spent considerable time communicating that we were in need of wine glasses and waiting for the staff to try to locate a pair. We ended up settling for two paper cups. Though the hotel was not of the high-class variety, it still came with a concierge who eagerly rode the elevator with us to bring us to our room. I think he simply wanted to eavesdrop on, or perhaps participate in, what appeared would be an enjoyable night. Five awkward floors later, and only after repeatedly being assured that we needed nothing else, the concierge left us alone at our room.

We enjoyed our bottle of red wine, which aided in loosening Boris's tongue, buying me some time to adjust to the fact that *holy crap, I'm in a private hotel room with a man I barely know!* We talked for a couple of hours—principally about God.

"You know, my religion would condemn me for being here with you now." My eyes met Boris's as I searched for approval to continue without being judged.

"Do you believe you should be condemned?" He held my gaze.

"Well, no. But I do believe in God. There is so much beauty in the world that I can't deny something larger than us has created it all." I paused before continuing, "So I try to follow his teachings. I figure if I live an honest, good life the majority of the time, a few sins will be overlooked, and I'll still go to heaven."

Boris waited for me to finish before revealing his perspective. "I used to believe in God, but growing up in Brazil I have seen so much suffering. Where is God in that? I prefer to just live my life as a good person and not worry about someone else's judgment. When I die, I die. That's it. At least my life will have offered some purpose while I was here."

"Really? You don't believe we have a spirit that lives on?"

"No, I don't. Our spirit just dies with our body. Death doesn't scare me. I like the idea of death. When my grandmother died last year, I asked my mother if I could keep her skull. I thought it would be so beautiful to have it to remember her by. She wouldn't let me, though."

"I'm not surprised." I laughed. "Where I come from, that would be considered sacrilege."

"Where I come from too," his words trailed off, revealing more similarities between us than we'd originally thought.

Speaking to Boris about my faith allowed me to feel known. If I was going to share the sacredness of my body with this man, I at least wanted him to know a piece of my soul.

Finally, the crutch of conversation that I'd been leaning on gave way to the reason we had placed ourselves in the hotel room to begin with. A look came across Boris's face that read, *It's time.* He silently picked me up and laid me across the bed, beginning to lift my denim dress above my waist. To add to my anxiety, I had my period and was ashamed of the blood. He assured me he loved blood. "I'm a vampire," he joked and reminded me that skulls and the night were his favorite things. In fact, a derivative of his middle name meant "pitch black" in Portuguese. *What have I gotten myself into?* I thought, *What if he really* is *a vampire?*

The tenderness of Boris's touch helped ease the knot of anxiety in the pit of my stomach. He caressed me ever so slowly along my legs, my abdomen, and my breasts. He stroked my face and looked into my eyes with compassion and care. He was searching for permission to enter my body. I did not wish to stop him. The act was not rushed; his entrance was slow and deliberate. I watched his head lean back in pleasure before returning his gaze to mine to check in with my own comfort and state of desire. I did not initiate movement, but I followed his lead with openness and trust. He would now be a part of my eternal memory—my story.

My quest for ecstasy was not found that night; I was too much in my head to relax and feel the sensations of my physical body. But I did feel nurtured, cherished, and broken open. This sex thing…it wasn't *so* scary. I still struggled with my insecurities around my inexperience. I felt like I was impersonating being a "real" woman.

"You were perfect," Boris assured me, as though reading my thoughts, stroking my hair behind my ear as we lay naked together in a peaceful state of relaxation.

I stared into his eyes and took in his words, but I didn't completely believe them. I thought perhaps he had created a fantasy in his mind about what it was like to be together. How could I have offered him pleasure? I hadn't done anything. But his words were encouraging, nonetheless. Perhaps I wasn't damaged after all.

We closed our eyes. I slept like a baby cradled in his arms, but my journey toward accepting myself as a woman had begun.

SUNDAY MORNING BEGAN slowly. We emerged from bed and checked out of the hotel to return to our hostel down the block. We walked in wearing the same clothes as the day before, and I wondered if anyone noticed. I felt slightly embarrassed and slightly proud. We indulged in our *dos medialunas* and made plans for our half-day together—Boris was flying back to Brazil that evening. I had been wanting to visit the neighborhood of La Boca—the supposed birthplace of the tango—but had been advised not to go alone, as it's not the safest area of the city. Boris agreed to join me.

We walked along Caminito hand in hand. The vibrant pastel buildings and European flavor of the neighborhood provided the perfect backdrop for a romantic farewell. We helped each other pick out colorful paintings done in the whimsical *fileteado* style. The art incorporates stylized lines and flowered, climbing plants that evoked poetic wonder within me. The paintings would serve as our relics of this day together.

Before long, Boris checked his watch. "I have to head back."

"I know," I replied regretfully.

"Have you seen the movie *Before Sunrise*?" Boris asked.

"Yes, that is one of my favorite movies!"

"Well, let's make a pact, like they did in the movie. Next year, if we still have feelings for each other, let's meet in Dublin for St. Patrick's Day."

The romantic in me loved the idea. "Deal!" I exclaimed.

With that decided, we took a taxi back to the hostel. Boris gathered his belongings, kissed me goodbye, and left to catch his flight.

The conversation that almost didn't happen, had I stayed within my shell while journaling about chocolate that first night at the hostel, ended up significantly impacting my future.

> *I write to you now in a completely different state of mind than any other time on this trip. To recall the first couple of weeks in Mendoza and Bariloche seems so long ago. My time in Buenos Aires has been surreal. I became a different person here. The name Buenos Aires will always bring back feelings of pleasure, nostalgia, and undefinable emotions. I still have over two weeks left. I don't know what to expect. My plans were so laid out. Now, it doesn't matter. All those lists of places to see have suddenly become less significant; my preference to see them alone has been shattered.*
>
> *Various places will bring back memories from only the last few days. How can 4 1/2 days completely change me like this? How can I let myself go so quickly and yet have it happen so naturally? I went with my instinct and did what it told me. Or, as Boris said, "You have this strong life force inside you that you call God." I've always thought it was God. I still believe that. But maybe I do have an inner force and strength of my own as well. I'd like to think that last night was meant to be, because I was relying on my instinct "from God" to tell me if it was right or not. I have no regret.*

3
Sex in Buenos Aires

BORIS WOULD BE my only sexual partner in Buenos Aires, but I was not without sex after he left. The city itself had a strong sexual vibe. Buenos Aires is the birthplace of the tango, after all. Like blues dancing, the sexual undertones of tango dancing cannot be denied. Is there anything more alluring to a man than a woman gliding across the floor in high heels, chest intimately pressed against his own, her legs wrapping around and between his legs in flirtatious play? Watching various tango performances during my visit, I was struck by how serious the female dancers' faces were as they engaged in the dance. They must remain a challenge for the males so that the men may hone their natural instinct for the hunt.

A woman will typically grant a man three consecutive dances in which he can prove his worthiness, as a dance partner and perhaps as a mate. He has limited opportunity, therefore, to pull out all the stops and translate them into intrigue and compatibility. Yes, women dancers know how to play the game, and the men grapple with the opportunity.

Nowhere is this cultural dance better executed than on the streets of Buenos Aires. Even when not dancing the tango, the women of Buenos Aires radiate sex, and the men are not afraid to acknowledge it. My features blended well with the local women's, and I learned to wear dresses, skirts, and heels to avoid standing out as a tourist. If I didn't open my mouth, I figured I was experiencing life as a typical Argentinean woman of my age and stature might. Of course, I may not have responded the way my counterpart would have.

Within every doorway on each block at least one man perched, uttering sexual slurs as I passed by. In my home culture, such actions are perceived as rude and offensive, so that is how I experienced them in Buenos Aires as well. I walked quickly, pretending I had not heard them, trying my best not to feel disgusted with their "perversion."

I learned that many Argentinean women, however, actually *enjoy* being the subject of such slurs. When they pass men and are *not* whistled at and sexually denoted, they are offended. I realize now that this is a perfect example of how everything is a matter of perception, but at the time I judged the women as not realizing the compromising position they were in. I did not feel I could pause alone anywhere in public for fear of being approached and propositioned. This fear kept me from ever truly being able to take a moment to appreciate stunning architecture or a street performance of the tango. However, *porteñas* walked with their heads held high, wearing much higher heels than I dared.

The men and women of Buenos Aires are also a lot more comfortable with physical affection and less in need of personal space than those in the culture I was raised in. The standard greeting is always a swift kiss on the cheek. This took me a long time to get used to, as at the time I energetically put up protective barriers even when someone I knew well would approach me for a hug. My physical inhibitions, obviously, extended well beyond the bedroom. If touch was not administered within my safety zone of the dance floor, I approached it with caution.

Though I found Argentina's comfort with physical touch and access to personal space refreshing and enviable, I found another aspect of the culture's relationship to the physical body quite sad. A very style-obsessed culture, the country has one of the highest rates of cosmetic surgery in the world. It is not uncommon for Argentineans to share that they've undergone plastic surgery for breast implants or nip-and-tuck treatments, and boob jobs are a popular birthday present from parents to beloved teenage daughters.

The culture may seem to lack introspection and effort to find happiness from within, but Argentina is a world leader in the practice of soul searching. There is no taboo in sharing that one goes to psychoanalysis two to three times per week—in fact, it is seen as "chic."

It is also chic to wear clothes touting phrases in the English language, even if one does not know what they mean. I recall with great amusement an evening at a high-end restaurant with several new Argentinean friends and one American friend. One of the Argentinean women was proudly wearing a T-shirt with a large red heart and giant letters reading, *Manual Love.*

"Nice shirt." The American male at the table laughed as he gestured to the young woman.

"Thank you," she replied with humility.

"Wait, you do know what it means, right?" He appeared surprised that she hadn't offered even a sly smile in response. She nervously looked down at her shirt, as if she had not yet considered what it might mean. She admitted perhaps she wasn't *quite* sure, to which he and I erupted in giggles as he explained its true meaning.

"Oh, perfect!" She exclaimed, with not a hint of embarrassment.

It would have been out of place to wear the shirt at such an establishment in the US, but there, it fit right in with the idea that English was posh, and sex—or masturbation—wasn't shameful. Besides, by now I had learned that sex wasn't as taboo in other parts of the world as it was in the world I'd grown up in—especially the one within my own head.

I could learn a lot from Buenos Aires.

4
A Reunion at Iguazú Falls

To: Rebecca
From: Boris
Subject: thoughts
I'm really passing through a hard time in my life now, emotionally speaking. Breaking up such an intense and long-term relationship like mine is not an easy thing. I can't believe I was thinking about you while I was having a discussion with her. Each time I thought about the bad times I had with her, I thought about how it would be if I was with you. Instead of being here drinking wine and fighting, why wasn't I in Buenos Aires talking to you about lindy hop and "contemporary blues"?

I've been thinking about you a lot. And now I'm not sure if both things are connected (fighting with her and thinking about you). I'm so confused...Should we really see each other again? Would it be good for us to do that? We both know that falling in love is a process; we know how it starts and how it develops, and how it ends. In this case, we are almost sure how it's going to end—you are going back to the US to live your life, and I will stay in Brazil. So, should we take the opportunity to have this intense experience together, to go deeper even knowing that it will be suddenly interrupted? Or, should we take it easy and accept that it would be better that we cool down and try to forget about all that stuff?

Please help me with your opinion. It's very important; it's about us. I'm really afraid of falling in love with you now.

BORIS AND I shared countless online chats, e-mails, and

video calls while I was still in Buenos Aires. We debated making plans to see each other again. We finally decided to risk the pain that might follow our inevitable departures. We didn't need to wait until Dublin the following year—we had one more week before I left South America. I boarded an overnight bus from Buenos Aires to Iguazú Falls, on the border with Brazil, where Boris would meet me at the bus station the following day.

> *I am now on the bus to Iguazú Falls. I am so thankful that this time I have someone to greet me once I arrive with open arms and great anticipation. I don't know if I could have emotionally dealt with taking this final trip alone. I require such a balance of personal time and time connecting with someone else.*
>
> *It is starting to sink in that next week I will be leaving this country behind. Though ultimately I know I am ready and have seen all the things I wanted to see, a large part of me is really sad to think about ending this brief but significant era of my life. What an experience this has been! I think of the person I have been here—a strong, independent, vulnerable, free woman.*
>
> *Sometimes I've wanted nothing more than to crawl inside myself and evaporate, so that I might avoid a language I can't express myself in or an unwelcome glare from a man on a street corner. Other times I walk confidently down the street with my head held high, feeling unstoppable and beautiful. Whatever emotion I have had, however, I am happy to realize I have faced head on.*

> *When I think about returning to the States, I think about who I was right before I left—certainly not a woman who dealt with her deepest emotion. Of course, I struggled to consider myself a "woman" at all. It doesn't seem like that long ago, yet I've had this whole period of an alternate life. I feel like I've been living in a dream world these last couple of months, and next week I will have to wake up, and I'll wonder if all of this really happened. Did all of these people really exist in my life? Do* they *remember me? Was I in* their *dreams?*

MY DREAM WORLD had only just begun. My bus pulled into the station the following morning. Boris's flight had arrived the night before. I remember looking out the window and finding him instantly. His long, curly hair was let down, and he was wearing a red T-shirt, shorts, and sandals. He was pacing, trying to gauge where the bus would stop. Our eyes met through the window. Yes, I was enamored and excited to get off the bus. However, part of me wanted to crawl to the back of the bus and pretend I'd never been on it; that was some other girl he'd seen through the window.

I had moved back into fear. I saw the intensity of the way he looked at me, and I was afraid, mostly of hurting him. I thought that perhaps I wasn't who he thought I was—someone who was more capable of feeling love and heightened emotion than I thought myself to be. I knew I had energetically pushed men away from me over the years because of my fear of sex, yes, but also because I was afraid they would get attached to me—and that I wouldn't be able to fall in love with them in return. After Ryan, I certainly worried about that.

Plus, I had been single for so long that I had manifested a false sense of pride around that fact. *Yeah, I'm single! I don't need a man. I am strong and independent!* Pretending to love being single was how I survived high school and college amid the sea of couples; I told myself I was exorbitantly happy as a single person—and had chosen this state—in the process of trying to convince others so that they would not feel pity for me. I was actually ashamed of always being the single one—the third or sometimes fifth wheel—so I claimed to prefer remaining single.

For all those reasons, locking eyes with Boris's that morning, I felt my protective walls begin to build again. My defense mechanisms rose from the knot of fear in my stomach and sought release: my eyes averted his, my tongue prepared apathetic words like a chemist concocting poison.

I stepped down from the bus and into his arms. I had to admit, I did feel good in his arms.

We walked inside the station and sat at the café; I was quite hungry after the eighteen-hour bus ride. While in my relationship with Ryan, I perfected the habit of staring intently and with great interest at something in the distance rather than engaging in eye contact with him. He had occasionally called me out on it. "Sometimes I feel like you don't want to be here with me," he would accuse. I would then give a detailed description of why something in the direction of my gaze was quite interesting and, in fact, he should have been looking at it too. I couldn't just admit that I wanted to be anywhere but where I was. I felt myself start to do this with Boris, but I realized it was merely out of habit—and, of course, fear. By the end of our meal, I had relaxed. *This is a different man. And I am a different woman.*

We left the café and checked into our hostel—this time we had a private room. The large window overlooked a backyard abundant with flowers and other foliage that provided our gaze an array of color. The maid was hanging sheets to dry in the sunlight.

"Oh, let me close the curtains," Boris moved toward the window to afford us more privacy.

"No, leave them open." I placed my hand on his arm with an unexpected sense of urgency. Boris looked at me with surprise.

"I enjoy the natural light." I offered an excuse for my reaction. It was true, but the greater truth was that I wanted to bask in the fantasy of being seen here, with this man. I wanted a witness to the beauty of this unlikely couple. In the eyes of an outsider, I must be perceived as beautiful, sexy, and worthy enough to be in a private room with an attractive man.

"Okay," Boris conceded with a somewhat curious look on his face and moved back to the bed, where he began unpacking his belongings. He pulled out a hardcover book with a puppy on the cover and excitedly approached me.

"I got you a small gift. It's the book I told you about, *Marley and Me.*"

He had found an English copy of the book for me in São Paulo and had written on the inside cover:

From: Boris
To: "Rebby"
I hope you enjoy it as much as I did!
Boris Ramirez, From Brazil

Who doesn't love a man who loves puppies? I found it funny that he'd written *From Brazil* after his name. As if I could possibly forget this man.

We began to refer to our time together in Iguazú Falls as our honeymoon. My memories indeed conjure up feelings of romantic bliss set against the most stunning backdrop.

We spent a full day exploring Iguazú National Park by foot, boat, and train. One of the great natural wonders of the world, the falls at Iguazú are three times the length of Niagara Falls and among the widest in the world. The climate is subtropical; it was the first time I'd been in a jungle. There were monkeys in the wild—I was enthralled by the feeling of walking through a zoo without cages. Butterflies swarmed us and precariously landed on my legs, in my hair, and on my outstretched hand. Across the falls, I could see Brazil. As a rather idealistic child, I had written countless reports on the necessity of saving the Brazilian rainforest. It was surreal to see it with my own eyes—and to take it in with a dashing Brazilian man by my side. *How did I get so lucky?* I marveled with joy.

After walking the length of the park, we decided to take a boat trip right up to the falls. We undressed to our swimsuits to spare our clothes from getting soaked—we had observed that the guides loved drenching tourists. Ever since seeing a clip from *Blue Lagoon* as a teenager, I'd associated waterfalls with eroticism. Then, I had a curious desire to stand beneath a powerful waterfall and lure men in for what I could only imagine would become a steamy sexual experience, though I could not visualize any level of detail. I'd never allowed myself to see the whole movie—I was too embarrassed to admit even to myself that I was that intrigued.

We were not allowed to enter the water at the national park, anyway. Regardless, my body resonated with the power and intensity of this natural creation, which complemented the emotional intensity that was unfolding between Boris and me. I could still feel myself holding back, but I was opening myself up to the possibility—and my own capability—of feeling a deeper range of emotions. I understood this was a temporary experience we were having together, but I think that very fact was what allowed me to crack open my shell. It was safe for me to let go, because the threat of attachment was not available to us once we returned to our respective countries. I would know I was capable of being desired and feeling attracted to another, yet I would not have to compromise myself long-term in order to appease someone else.

And so our weekend continued; we engaged in playfulness in the hostel swimming pool, at the Ping-Pong table, and in bed. I woke up one morning and initiated sex for the first time in my life. I experienced desire, and I bravely pursued it. Once the act would begin, however, I'd surrender completely to his movements. I was still not confident enough to explore my own sexual expression. We showered together afterward; it was more intimate of an experience than the sex itself, as we were more cognizant of the details of each other's bodies after having released the intensity of our physical hunger. We began a new ritual of brushing our teeth together; it was a simple routine I could imagine doing with him forty years later. It felt that natural.

Once as we made love, with his long, curly hair let down, loose strands sticking to his face in perspiration, and a faraway look in his eyes, I thought, *What am I doing here?* But I just as likely meant, *What is* he *doing here?* I felt so far removed from the version of myself that I was familiar with. I felt like a "bad" girl. It felt good.

I didn't open myself up solely on a physical level; I remember sharing with him some details of the relationship I had left behind in Nashville. I was still too ashamed to admit that Ryan was the only other person I had ever been with—at twenty-five I felt old enough that there "should" have been several—but I did share that I was struggling with feeling inadequate as a woman. He did his best to assure me that I was a beautiful and mature woman, but it was still hard for me to understand how he could believe that. (I still got overly excited every time we passed an ice cream shop.) But I was on my way, I knew.

One night I began to think about my upcoming cross-country drive, moving my belongings from La Crosse to

Portland. Though I knew that I would be fine, I had my moments of intense fear. Lying in bed that night with Boris, I felt my mind lose control as it began to consider every possible thing that could go wrong; he caressed me and held me, and though he offered me consoling words, he did not try to control my emotion or halt it. He could stay with it. I knew then that I was being given a beautiful gift.

I anticipated that parting ways on Monday would be difficult. Boris was originally going to fly home Sunday night, but he didn't feel right about leaving me alone my final night; he wanted to see me safely to the bus station Monday afternoon. The next available flight for him was early Tuesday morning; he would have to find a café to work from on Monday, as he had an important conference call to attend. Finding both a quiet café and a strong internet connection in a small Argentinean town was easier said than done, but he eventually managed. He politely asked for space from me so he could focus on his call. It was challenging to sit apart from him; I wanted to touch him and take in his presence while I still could.

Later, we left the café and found a hostel closer to town for him to stay at for the night. As he used the bathroom, I took the opportunity to slip a note under his pillow. *I miss you already. —Rebby.*

From the hostel, we took a taxi to the bus station. We silently held hands in the backseat; our minds were consumed with the question and wonder of if we would ever see each other again. I would board my flight from Buenos Aires to Minneapolis in just a few days; from there I would be displaced even farther as I moved to Portland. The future was unknown. We squeezed each other's hands tighter. Only one phrase seemed appropriate to exchange.

"Thank you."

"Thank *you.*"

We kissed goodbye, and he watched me board the bus. This time, meeting his eyes from my seat in the back of the bus, I felt no fear. My only regret: that our time together on this journey had come to an end. The long bus ride back would provide welcome space for contemplation.

> *I am coming off a really great weekend. God is beginning to challenge me. He is challenging me to let myself go. Emotionally, physically…to be the woman I know I can be. I am in that precarious stage between young adult and "mature" adult. I am starting, slowly but unmistakably, to open myself up. To love, to passion, to pain, to fear, to vulnerability, to acceptance, to struggle, and to achievement. I can recognize risk, yet not back down because of it. I will allow myself to feel, be it pain or pleasure, as long as it makes me better or stronger in the end.*
>
> *I allowed myself to connect with someone else. Intimately, emotionally, physically, knowing we will have to leave each other. Not knowing what the future would hold. But knowing it was okay…I would be all right. Whatever happens, I will never forget Boris. He's "my Brazilian," one of a small group of people who have shaped me, and in such a short time. I believe there*

is a good chance we will see each other again—in the US or Brazil—but if we don't, it's because the purpose we were to serve to each other has already been planted, and maybe it's up to ourselves, or someone else, to continue to nurture it.

I have been blessed to cross his path. And I do hope I have left a positive mark on his life.

To: Rebecca
From: Boris
Subject: Thank you
Can you believe there was dust in my eyes the exact moment that the bus left? :)

Rebby, I would just like to say THANK YOU... for your caress, for your sweetness, for your smile. For talking to me, for making me laugh, for making me happy. For trusting me and for sharing a part of your life with me.

I think you're a VERY SPECIAL WOMAN (not a very special GIRL, okay? :)), and thus I feel also special for your accepting me being with you for a while.

I'll miss you.

5
Finding a New Home

RETURNING TO MY parents' home after such a transformative adventure was challenging. My heart was still in Argentina with Boris. I allowed in old triggers, some petty, others with roots that ran deep. I remember feeling frustrated that I felt I had to hide the true nature of my relationship with Boris. That it would have been shameful, at least from my parents' perspective, to have slept with someone I wasn't married to, let alone someone I'd just met.

I figured they assumed there was a bit more than just friendship enveloping the relationship, as it was impossible to hide the fact that I was often chatting on the computer and then staying up late at night to make video calls. One day, Boris lost his wireless connection mid-chat, and called my parent's home phone line to let me know what had happened. My mom answered the phone; I couldn't escape an introduction, "Hi, I'm Rebecca's friend, Boris." I let her speak to him for a few minutes before she correctly interpreted my glare as a demand to hand the phone over. I was embarrassed, but also amused that my mom seemed to really enjoy talking to him. Though she always cautioned no sex before marriage, she did delight in fantasizing about boys in her daughter's life.

My mom and dad both wanted to see their daughter married off to a respectable man. That I had a boyfriend would be a relief to them. When I was a teenager, my mom questioned me about my sexuality. I never spoke of any boys or brought anyone home, so…was I perhaps a *lesbian*? She tried to reassure me that she'd still love me and, of course, well, there was nothing *wrong* with being a lesbian, really…but it was not hard to see past her considerable fear. I assured her that she need not worry, but I don't think she was truly convinced. It didn't help that my prom "date" was a female friend, though she, like me, was going stag not by preference but by circumstance. Some of my senior pictures even included a pose with my best friend, a girl who had a masculine stature. My aunt looked at the photo with a grin and a wink, inquiring, "And who is *he*?"

From a general standpoint, my parents simply wanted what they thought was best for their daughter. I never doubted their love and for the most part received their unrestricted support of my endeavors. But that was relatively easy—I was a "good kid." I left little opportunity for them to need to redirect my path. I got straight As in school, had no dating escapades to cause them to enforce a curfew, and preferred reading and writing to loud music and too much TV.

When I did watch TV, even as a teenager, it was usually Country Music Television, a rather wholesome channel, which although it wasn't affiliated with a particular religion, often featured songs that preached God-fearing Christian dogma and traditional family values. So when my dad came home from work one night to find his eighteen-year-old daughter watching a music video of a "bedroom scene" depicting an affair, I was met with the overly anxious exclamation of, "What the *hell* is this? Turn that off, right now!"

Though I was still in high school, I was technically an adult, and I was mad that my dad still felt he had to censor things for me—as if watching a Garth Brooks video equated with watching an X-rated movie. I stormed up to my room to fret about the predicament I was in, trapped in the body of a young woman, considered a child by the standards of my parents and even my own inherent beliefs about myself that had just now been reinforced by my dad's reaction.

Seven years later, back at my parents' home after years of independence and self-discovery, I at times still suffocated in the old energy of who I'd been when I'd lived full-time with them. My parents, after all, didn't really *know* me anymore. I had gone off to Nashville and then to Argentina and returned to their home as a liberal vegan (which I had warned them about), no longer a virgin (which I wasn't so directly open about), who was beginning to question her Christian faith (they couldn't help but sense it). They wanted so badly to know me, yet that desire contributed to my pushing them further away.

I didn't feel safe sharing my new self with them, believing I'd be drilled with fervent rebuttals and disappointment that I wasn't turning out quite the way they'd intended. Of course, I wasn't doing a great job of presenting my viewpoints to their opposition: being back in my old hometown sparked an adolescent streak of rebellion and defensiveness I hadn't displayed as an actual adolescent. And so it was that before leaving for Portland, I engaged in several heavy political debates with my dad and one colossal fight with my mom.

The fight's topic was trivial, but the emotion behind it was profound. I had invited a friend of mine, who was also a colleague of my mom's, over for afternoon tea. My mom was home on her lunch hour when I told her of the upcoming visit.

"She is coming *here*? *Now*?!" she exclaimed.

I was caught off guard by her heightened anxiety, "Yes..." I answered tentatively. "What's the big deal?"

"Look at the house! We can't have guests with it looking like this! You have to call her—tell her you'll meet her someplace else."

"I can't call her now—it's too late. She's probably already on her way. It's no big deal, Mom. She won't even notice the clutter."

"I can't believe you invited a colleague of mine over without telling me in advance." She paced about the living room, gathering strewn jackets and stacking magazines. Tears laced her eyes, but I selfishly ignored their implication. I thought I was the one being wronged.

The hidden reason for her reaction was revealed before long, "I wish you were closer to me, Rebecca. I wish you trusted me. Why can't you tell me more about what goes on in your life?"

I could have responded with love. I could have received her truth with compassion and understanding and allowed a pathway for a greater bond between a mother and her only daughter. But instead I reacted from my own fear—that allowing her to be close to me meant sacrificing personal power.

"I *can't* open up with you, Mom! You overreact to everything I say." I felt suffocated by her love, though I couldn't articulate that at the time.

I recalled the times I told my mom about hurtful things my friends had done or said when I was in middle and high school. My mom's emotion was highly visible in the expression on her face and the tone of her voice as she responded to my pain. "You need to find different friends!" she'd say with conviction, followed with the questions, "Are you depressed? Do you need to see a psychologist?" Though I understood her reaction was one of deep sadness that her daughter was hurting, its extremity kept me from feeling understood or wanting to share more. Expressing any emotion other than happiness felt precarious.

My mom eventually gave in to my friend coming over for tea. Together, we cleaned the house with the few minutes we had left before she had to leave for work. It hurt to see my mom upset, but I still wasn't ready to admit my role.

I vented to Boris about the argument while chatting online later that evening. I'd expected to be met with the agreement that I was right; however, I was instead challenged to see my role in creating the conflict and my responsibility in healing it. Really, the fight was not so much about the current state of my mother's home but my lack of understanding for the values that were important to her—including a loving and close relationship with her daughter.

I was unable, or unwilling, to see that truth at that time in my life. I demanded to be "right," so, as we're typically taught from a young age, someone else must be "wrong." I hadn't yet discovered that multiple people could be "right" (and that when we all accept complete responsibility within our relationships, *that* is when our world begins to change). Boris's suggestion of my responsibility triggered me, probably because I intrinsically knew there was truth in what he said, but my ego did not yet want to accept that truth. I still believed the only real release from suffering was to avoid it—not move through it. Just as I had sought temporary escape in Argentina, I sought more permanent escape by living someplace new—where no one from my past could haunt me with their preconceived notions of who I was or who I should be. I still defined *home* as a place made up of external components of my existence—the place, the people, and the possessions that I claim as part of myself. I wanted my new home.

I remained at my parents' house—as I'd started thinking of it, not as my home—for ten days, waiting out both a case of mild bronchitis and a snowstorm. Finally, I was able to load my car with all of my belongings and begin the journey to Portland. Overall, I was thrilled at the concept of undertaking such an adventure by myself; I knew it would be empowering. I still had my moments of fear, as when I considered what could happen along the way. It felt reassuring to know that Boris, even all the way in

Brazil, was following my travels online. He called me occasionally as I drove, and each night after checking in to my hotel, I video chatted with him. I believe I would have been quite lonely at such a pivotal time of my life had I not had warm thoughts of him to occupy empty spaces of my mind.

Upon arriving in Portland, I located a shared apartment to sublet for my first two months. I was convinced my roommate was a vampire. He kept the shades drawn during the gorgeous weather and watched *Buffy the Vampire Slayer* all day. I was beginning to wonder if I had an intrinsic quality that attracted men who pretended to be vampires, or joked about being, as Boris had, into my life. I did not know it at the time, but the *Twilight* movies were then being filmed in and around Portland. I had even moved to a geographic environment in which vampires, apparently, thrived.

Still, I was content with my temporary living situation. I had always preferred having male roommates. Growing up, I took great pride in being considered "one of the guys." I attribute much of that reasoning to my older brother. I had wanted so desperately to gain his approval and affection, which I most often achieved by being knowledgeable about sports and an active participant in sports myself. He groomed me to be "tough"—a personality that I developed only when in male company, yet a matter of dress that I retained for all situations and environments (except gymnastics, and later dance). My brother picked out baggy clothes for me—following the latest trends of MC Hammer and Vanilla Ice—as well as hoodies and jackets touting his favorite sports teams. It was his way of expressing interest and love for his little sister. He wanted me to be seen as "cool." The style suited my goals at the time anyway, as it covered my developing feminine form.

I was a self-proclaimed tomboy and proud of it. It got me attention from boys, but I later realized it was also—aside from my being too innocent—what kept them from wanting to date me. Being "one of the guys" was not exactly the biggest turn-on. In high school study hall I would approach boys I was interested in with my favorite line: "Wanna arm wrestle?" The only way I knew how to communicate with boys was the way I did with my brother.

After high school I sought male company more than I did female. I was tired of the games my girlfriends had played in my school years—the gossip, the competition for boys and for reaching the next "base." I couldn't relate. I couldn't even talk about getting PMS—my periods were artificial. Boys were better company; they were easier. If I could talk sports, we could be friends. Besides, living with men and having mostly male friends allowed me to complement my natural feminine energy with the masculine energy I so strongly craved from men but in a safe environment: myself, and strictly platonic male friends. I knew they wouldn't pursue me; they just wanted to hang out with me on the couch and watch the game.

Or in this case, watch *Buffy*.

I paid my "vampire" roommate little mind. I was busy searching for a job by day and exploring the

Portland dance scene by night. The blues-dancing scene in Nashville was very underground when I'd lived there, as the city was in the Bible Belt, after all. The first time I saw blues dancing was literally underground, in a basement—well, my basement. When I was living with Micah and two other men from the dance scene, we were hosting a dance party. As the night wore on, the lights progressively dimmed, the music slowed, and the dancers moved in closer together.

I was embarrassed to watch them; I felt like I was invading a very private moment. Until then, I'd only seen such seductive dancing in the movies. My conscience struggled with justifying the morality of what I was seeing; the sexual undertones of the dance brought my awareness to my own sexuality and feeling of incompetence, and though I was intrigued by how the dancers were moving, I immediately labeled it "not for me."

Micah offered me blues dance lessons, and it was then that I learned that the dance is about partnership, connection, and self-expression. Well, really, it's about what you want it to be about, and those characteristics happened to be what I craved at that time in my life. I would later see this style of dance at lindy exchanges I attended in the more progressive Southern cities of Atlanta, Georgia, and Asheville, North Carolina. The later in the night, the slower the music, paving the way for jazz tunes to transmute into soulful blues melodies. Thus began my love affair with this sensual and spiritually rooted style of dance.

But it wasn't until I moved to Portland that I really began to immerse myself in the dance. I had not known before moving there that the blues and tango scenes in Portland are among the best in the world. I also discovered a growing movement called fusion that melds lindy hop, blues, and tango beautifully into one. It was a magic triune, for me—breaking all categorical rules to create new avenues of self-expression.

All three styles, separately or together, offered a safe place for me to express my sensuality and enjoy being touched. I don't know where I'd be today without dance. How wonderful it would be if schools incorporated more dance instruction into the curriculum; the etiquette and lessons in partnership and communication that dancing naturally teaches can be applied in all relationships. I believe that the state of sexual repression that our society suffers would be greatly reduced if we were simply encouraged to dance.

Despite connecting with the local dance scene, I had yet to establish a sense of belonging in Portland. Part of me was still longing to remain in my past.

> *Whenever I am allowed down time, life suddenly becomes more complicated. How can I be so strong that I can endure nearly two months in a foreign country traveling alone, and then come back to the States and endure a thirty-hour drive cross-country alone, only to reach my destination and then feel lonely?!*
>
> *It's sinking in that this dream world I've been living in has to come to an end...that it pretty much already has. I was looking at pictures from Iguazú Falls tonight, and I can't believe that was only two weeks ago. It seems a world away—it is a world away! My life*

as it existed two weeks ago no longer exists—and will never again exist. I am suddenly scared. Scared that this next life will be so lonely. Scared that the people I've connected with in my past life may be gone forever.

Why is it that I feel I have such unfinished business with Boris? I feel like we'll see each other again, but really, how can I be so sure? And how can I know either of us won't be with someone else at that time? I want to believe I can show him a better, more beautiful, more mature side of me, because he deserves it. I want to believe I will be able to get to know him better…there is much more depth to his personality that I want to explore. I think I can learn a lot from him. I really miss him. And I'd like to give myself to him in ways I wasn't ready to before. I want to show him all of me—to confidently express myself sexually with him, and be honest about my insecurities. I'm not sure I'm ready now, but I am hopeful that one day I will be.

BORIS AND I continued to chat online and via video calls regularly for my first few months in Portland. Gradually, however, the physical distance generated an emotional disconnect. I started to wonder if what I thought I'd felt before had been "real." Was I simply caught up in the fantasy of a romance movie? Girl travels world, meets sexy Brazilian man, love affair ensues—but will distance keep them apart?

We agreed, however, that distance did seem to win—at least for now. We didn't want to keep each other from living our lives. He would need to undergo a lengthy application process to obtain a visa to come to the United

States. Of course, even a short visit to Brazil or the United States would cost money we did not have. Perhaps we needed to just accept that what we'd had together had been beautiful, albeit temporary, and we'd forever carry the memories in our hearts.

I tried to keep my passion for foreign languages and cultures alive by enrolling in a certification program for teaching English as a foreign language. I felt that such expertise could help me find meaningful work, if not locally then abroad—perhaps back in Argentina? I wasn't ready to let go of the dream world the country had allowed me to entertain.

In the meantime I needed some sort of work. But I had become so disheartened at the prospect of tailoring yet another cover letter and resume to a job that held no intrinsic meaning to me. Held up against the vivaciousness of traveling abroad—the exotic rapture of a foreign culture and language, and the taste of an international love—my new life lacked significant appeal. With each job interview, I sank into greater despair. I couldn't bear the thought of accepting an entry-level office position, no matter how temporary. I exhausted my savings, sold the beloved guitar I kept on hand more for musically inclined friends than I did for myself, and just when I was down to my last dollar, my persistence paid off and I was offered a job at a place I'd had hopeful sights on since before moving to Portland—the historic Aladdin Theater.

I began working part-time at the concert venue, which now played host to some of my favorite musicians, including Patty Griffin, Emmylou Harris, and Marc Cohn.

Working the latter's show one early summer evening, I listened thoughtfully as he closed the performance with "Walking in Memphis."

The lyrics brought me back to my days in Tennessee. I stood in the back of the theater, eyes closed, the sights and sounds of the South coursing back within my synapses. I began to reminisce on the joy I felt while working at the Ryman Auditorium in Nashville. Standing in the balcony of the Mother Church of Country Music, I had some of the most powerful spiritual experiences of my life. I listened to the smooth molasses of Norah Jones's voice crooning "Come Away with Me," melted within the Black Crowes' soulful lament "She Talks to Angels," and escaped inside yet another ethereal experience guided by Bonnie Raitt and her guitar with her celestial serenade "Angel from Montgomery."

I would lean back with my eyes closed, a smile gracing my face, and silently realize with gratitude, *There is no place in the world I'd rather be.* Music moved me. At a time when my emotions were numb to physical touch and shielded from vulnerability, I allowed myself to be innately touched and transported by soulful melodies.

My experience working at the Ryman led me to pursue a job at a similar music venue in Portland, and I was so grateful to be given the opportunity to become part of the Aladdin family. It truly felt like a family, and the music made me feel like I had found a new home.

Despite the comfort my new job provided me, I felt instinctively called to revisit Nashville. Ryan still had a presence in my life. He would call me on occasion, and I felt trapped into talking to him—I still found it so hard to block his supplications for a friend, for me to be a decent human being. He just wanted to talk…couldn't I at least listen?

I also greatly missed the familiar faces of the dance scene in Nashville, especially Micah. I craved seeing him again upon my return to the city. I wanted to show him who I'd become since he'd last seen me. Argentina had changed me. I wanted to share with him that I was no longer so innocent…that it had been worth breaking the rules to be with me. I felt I had something to prove.

Aside from seeking closure on the escapades with males I'd engaged in within the city's trenches, I also knew my body was holding on to another memory from my time there that I'd tried hard to suppress. Several reasons—some romantic, some violent—led me back to Nashville. I had some serious roots to dig up from the soil.

6
Saying Goodbye in Nashville

BY MOVING TO Nashville after college, leaving the environment in which I'd been raised to stay under someone else's rules—be they my parents', my teachers', or my priest's—I was able to clearly consider that the rules were now solely my own, and therefore the consequences were exclusively a result of my own creation.

I took full responsibility for my choices. Thus, I never labeled myself a victim during my relationship with Ryan. Perhaps he did "use" me, but could I conceivably also have used him? For example, I was ashamed of being a virgin. He relieved me of the humiliation I felt around that particular fact. I could also say that I "used" him to prove I was worthy of being conditionally loved. In hindsight, I've been able to understand that it wasn't just me that was hurt, either. I carried an excessive degree of shame within me that undoubtedly projected onto him. How could it not? One person's pain unmistakably becomes another's. Our relationship was a two-way street, really, named Heal Me.

We were so young. We thought we were mature and wise, but we were not. We traded each other, one damaged part for another. We projected the pain from our youth, the punishments of our parents, and the perilous seeds of mounting expectation and resentment onto each other, without conscious knowledge of what we were doing. I wanted him to love me without wanting sex from me. He wanted me to prove my love for him by having sex with him. Of course, we couldn't both get what we wanted. Someone had to lose. At the time, I thought the only loser was me.

I'd been taught not to place my needs above those of another. God commanded it; my mother demonstrated it. What began as someone else's rule became my own self-imposed rule. I would submit to everything from social visits I preferred not to engage in to sex with my partner when I did not want it. This rule left me with no voice. Though I felt disconnected from my real truth and desire when I made such choices, I was able to bury the feeling by telling myself that when I woke up the next day, it would all be over. I was, after all, the only one being "hurt" by my choices.

I managed this charade until an incident within my last six months in Nashville forced me to really pay attention. I was not the only one being hurt. It was a wakeup call for me that I *had* to find my voice.

Before moving in with my dancer roommates, I shared a house with two women. One morning while I was taking a shower upstairs, I heard a noise coming from the kitchen. One of my roommates had been home when I stepped in the shower, so I did not suspect anything strange. I did not know that she had already left.

I took my time drying off and getting dressed, all along hearing noises from the kitchen. I knew my roommate was getting ready to go camping, and I assumed she was simply preparing her gear. I started down the steps, contemplating what I would have for breakfast, when I was stopped in my tracks. I could see a man holding a long kitchen knife, attempting to break through the glass back door. I froze. Our eyes met. He froze as well—I don't know if it was because he had not expected anyone to be home or because he had expected to be inside before confronting me. I can't tell you how many moments passed; it felt like an eternity before he turned to run for the bike he had left lying on the ground.

In my state of shock, I did not even think to call the police. He was gone—what could they do? I instead called my roommate. She was in a more coherent state of mind and offered to call the police as she turned around to drive back home. I paced back and forth, nervously glancing out the window, shaking. When my roommate arrived, we sat together on the front steps, waiting for the police to arrive. Three police cars passed our house within the next hour—none of them stopping—before the one that was sent in response to our call finally pulled into our drive.

We sat in the kitchen as paperwork was filled out, and I gave my best description of what the man had looked like. He was tall with a strong build, African American, bald, perhaps late forties. His eyes…I remembered his eyes. I couldn't describe them, but I would know them if I saw them.

I was not comfortable staying at my home. Immediately after the officers and my roommate left, I sought refuge with Ryan, who lived just down the street. I told him what happened, and he listened with what seemed like feigned interest. I couldn't believe he was not more empathetic. I was hurt by his indifference but did not consider leaving to stay with another friend. I think I felt that he "owed" it to me to protect me. If he still expected me to satisfy his needs, was I not at least worthy of his protection?

Not two hours had passed before I received a call from the police department. They believed they had found the perpetrator; could I identify him? I went to the scene of his capture, two blocks from my house. The man was in the backseat of the police car, his broken bicycle strewn a few feet away on the train tracks. The cops had driven into him to stop his escape. The window was rolled down; I was brought within two feet of him. He looked me in the eye as I held his gaze only momentarily.

"Yes, that's him." I shook with discomfort. I knew nothing of proper criminal procedures, but I knew this method of identification felt wrong. I shouldn't have had to face him like this—for both my own sake and his. It was like looking an injured animal in the eye while directing to another, "Yes, this one here. Make him suffer." I knew that though I was perceived as the "victim," he was too. What had brought him to attempt to commit this crime? I don't even know what his intention was. What hurt him so much that he felt he had to hurt me? Or steal from me? Or God only knows what.

I stood around for about half an hour, waiting for the officers to let me know I could leave. They leafed through a manual—trying to determine what to charge him with. They decided on attempted burglary. They regretfully informed me that they could not detain him for this charge;

they could merely take down his information, fine him, and release him.

What? Just like that, he would be released? My God, thanks to this long process of identification and loitering around the vehicle he sat in, he could very well identify *me* now. And I was supposed to "go on home and *relax*"? No way!

I returned to Ryan's house, where I would spend the week figuring out where I would live next. My two roommates had already made plans for temporary housing of their own. I knew I could never return to live at that house, not with this man back out on the street. A neighbor had informed the officers that she knew the man. She had often seen him ride his bike across our yard, visiting his uncle who lived in our cul de sac. He was sure to be back in the neighborhood, and I'd be damned if I'd be there to cross paths with him again.

I heard that my dance teacher's house was looking for a fourth roommate. I explained the urgency of my situation and asked that I move in as soon as possible. Within the week, I had a new home, neighborhood, and roommates.

A few more days passed before I again heard from the police department. They had inaccurately charged him; the knife was a weapon, and he should have been charged with attempted aggravated burglary. Jail time was in order. This certainly felt more appropriate for the crime, yet anger set in that it wasn't properly handled in the first place. Perhaps I wouldn't have felt the need to move had it been. The police went to the man's home address and rearrested him, placing him into the county jail, where he would wait until the court date, set for two months later. I would need to attend as a witness to his crime. I cringed at the thought of having to see him again.

That day my stomach housed a knot of twisted anxiety as I waited for them to lead the man into the courtroom. Twenty feet to my right, the door finally opened and a handcuffed man in orange was brought in and seated near the far wall.

Wait, is that…? He didn't look as I expected him to. Two months had passed. He had gained weight. And he seemed shorter.

"There's the motherfucker," the police officer leaned over and whispered to me. I was uncomfortable with his choice of words, yet his being a man in a position of authority made me nod my head in agreement. I sought affinity and rapport with him; I wanted to identify with the "good side." Don't police officers represent all things just? Safety? Security?

The officer was called up to the stand. Confidently, without even looking at the man on trial, he asserted that yes, this was the man he had caught, and subsequently released, for the crime in question on the aforementioned date. He spoke with such certainty, but that did not calm me.

In truth, he really didn't look like the man I had identified the day of the crime. I swallowed this realization, attempting to bury it in the deepest trenches of my soul. No one had to know it existed. My job was easy—I simply had to follow the officer who already laid claim to this man being the perpetrator and agree, "Yes, that is him." For all I knew, it *was* him, right? I didn't know what they fed prisoners—perhaps he really was keen on it and had simply just gained weight. *Something* about him did seem familiar.

I took the stand. As I was asked to identify the man in the courtroom who had committed this crime against me, I looked at the man in question. He did not look at me. His head hung as if he had already accepted a fate that he knew he had no control over. Not a trace of his body language portrayed an ounce of hope that I might somehow be his savior. "Yes, that is the man." My mouth was dry, but I managed to release the words everyone in the room expected me to say. My statement was perceived as a matter of formality. My job was done; I could leave.

I felt sick. I stepped into the elevator and ended up riding down with the officer on my case as well as the lawyer representing the criminal. The lawyer greeted me warmly.

"I'm sorry you had to go through that. Son of a bitch kept saying it wasn't him, that it was his brother. Can you believe that?"

I forced a smile in feigned appreciation for his "support."

Wait. *His brother,* I thought. Could that be? Was that angle investigated? My train of thought was interrupted.

"Well, I'm just glad we caught him again. Good to see him behind bars." The officer seemed to want to pat himself on the back for a job well done. Perhaps now he'd earn a gold star.

I said goodbye to both men and exited the elevator and the building as quickly as I could. I don't know how I made the drive home. I shook with panic and trepidation.

His brother, his brother…

I couldn't get the idea out of my head. Is that why an aspect of him seemed familiar? They would look somewhat alike, but not *exactly.* At last something the officer said on the day of the second arrest came to mind:

"He doesn't have his ID on him, but we got his social security number and looked him up." They'd found a series of minor criminal accounts in his past but nothing recent.

They never even checked his ID.

I do not want to completely ignore the fact that there were racial factors at play, nor do I want to explore those factors here. I'll just say that I am deeply saddened at the current state of our "progressive" nation, as well as the immensely flawed law enforcement system. We still have a long way to go.

I am not a runner, but that's what I did after returning home from the courtroom. It's my least favorite form of physical exercise, but it was the only thing I could think to do. The inside of my body was tormented by the sudden belief, the absolute *knowing* that the man I had just helped convict was innocent. I had stood and sworn before a judge that I would say "the whole truth and nothing but the truth, so help me God," and I had *lied.* I wanted to run away from myself.

Open mouth, insert shame. Buckets of it. Now, pack it down in there, real good and tight, and store it there for years. My body became an affordable housing district for not only shame but its close relatives: guilt and embarrassment. And once they settled in, Great-Granddaddy Fear was welcomed to the neighborhood as head of household.

What were the legal repercussions of lying in court? In my limited understanding of the legal system, I did not know then that I would likely be protected against charges should I step forward and say I had been wrong. Days passed before I summoned the courage to call the victim witness coordinator representing my case to share that I wasn't *absolutely* certain the man I had identified in court was the perpetrator. She responded with kindness and more competence than anyone else on the case seemed to have had.

A few months later, I heard from the district attorney's office. They had gone back to my old house and fingerprinted the door. The man convicted was indeed innocent—it had been his brother who had committed the crime and then passed the blame by skillfully reciting his innocent brother's social security number and other personal information. The correct brother was now in prison, having received a sentence of eight years for attempted aggravated burglary and criminal impersonation.

The legal system fixed "my" mistake, so I could rest easy, right? Wrong. I still felt an exorbitant degree of responsibility that a man had sacrificed months of his life in prison awaiting trial for a crime he didn't commit. I was exceedingly hard on myself that I didn't respond to my inner wisdom on the day of the trial and speak my truth: "Actually, I am not positive that is the man that committed this crime." Would it have been so hard? I couldn't forgive myself.

I was frustrated with law enforcement and the legal procedures, but what I could not let go of was my own responsibility in the situation. Yes, I was approached at my home by an ill-intentioned man bearing a weapon. I was shocked, scared, and upset…but I was not physically hurt. This man had committed an act for which there should be consequences, but I knew even then that I could decide if I wanted to be a victim. I chose instead to view myself as a villain. It was no more accurate to represent myself in the latter light, but I had not yet conceptualized that belief. My deeper spiritual study had not yet begun.

And so it was that I returned to Nashville, still feeling the burning memory of my role in a corrupt trial that had led to an innocent man's suffering. Still feeling unfinished business with my friends there, including my ex-roommate and my ex-boyfriend. Yet still unsure of what that unfinished business was exactly. Once there, however, it didn't take me long to figure it out.

My arrival at the Nashville airport was not how I envisioned it. My circle of dance friends used to coordinate giant parties to greet the return of other members of the dance community. I was not met with the actualization of such a cinematic reunion. I was fortunate to find a friend who agreed to pick me up and drop me off at the house where my three former roommates, including Micah, still resided.

Micah was away that first night, but I arranged an evening out with him the following night. I wanted to visit the old honky-tonks on Broadway, dance on their dirty floors muddied and scarred by legends of country music's past. But dancing and chatting with Micah weren't enough for me. I was still desperate to feel special—and that night I wanted him to fulfill that need for me. I tried to recreate the scene from New Orleans. I ordered us a couple rounds of shots. I could feel his hesitancy to get physical, but I pursued him nonetheless. My experience with Boris had elevated my confidence with men. One more drink, and he gave in.

We made out on the streets of downtown, and brought the energy back home with us. We had the house to ourselves that night and took advantage of the living room couch—to say we made love would not be accurate. We had fast, flippant sex. We didn't even make eye contact or consider sharing a bed for the remainder of the night. He sauntered off to his room downstairs, and I to mine above. We already regretted it. I felt I'd devalued not only myself but our friendship. I'd used him to make my ego feel less bruised. He meant more than that to me. And I knew I did to him too.

We didn't get any more time alone together after that night. The following day, we would each rise and depart at different times to attend a mutual friend's wedding in rural Tennessee. He approached me at the wedding reception and softly squeezed my shoulder. I knew what it meant. I hoped my gaze conveyed the same apology.

Ryan astounded me by not being interested in seeing me during my visit. He did give me a ride back to the airport. Without having to express it in words, I think we both felt that our communication would end there. It hurt to be around each other. We knew we couldn't rely on the other for healing...that was a dead-end road we'd traveled before. We needed to go our separate ways. We were fully ready for that now.

> *Here I am. Six months later, to the day, from the day I left this room. This house. This city that I had to escape from, to rediscover myself. I find it ironic that it almost feels like I never left...and yet here I lie, listening to the one CD I accidently left behind—Astor Piazzolla. Argentinean tango music. Reminding me that I did leave. That I now have an assortment of new, beautiful people and experiences in my life. Beautiful memories...perhaps already fading...but maybe to be rediscovered again at a later time.*
>
> *I know now that I did not come back here to reconnect with this life and these people in it. I came to say goodbye. I don't plan to come back for a very, very long time. And by that time, probably all of these people will be gone, and I will merely come to reconnect with the city itself, and memories left behind.*
>
> *I had craved coming back to Nashville this week. I believed I needed it. I guess I did need it, but not for the reasons I had thought or sought. I learned today that most of my friends here are friends of convenience, and*

my ex really isn't a friend at all. There's a saying that only once you leave somewhere and come back do you truly know it to begin with. I feel that way about people too. I needed to come back here to realize that I create my own culture. What beautiful freedom we have! I can decide what and who are important to me, and make up my life. I choose how I spend my time, where I visit, who I reveal myself to.

I think God wanted to teach me some important lessons this trip. He wanted to show me that happiness and love cannot be found in a particular place, but merely where you are. It has to be created. I am so thankful that I have this chance to "restart" my life. My life in Portland is clean, and I want to keep it that way. I want to avoid unhealthy relationships and environments that do not contribute to my being in a positive way. I am so happy to recognize that. And I pray that I can withhold my promises to myself as I have failed to do on this temporary lapse back into this past version of me. Wow, only six months can create a whole new version of self!

I am sure there will be much more to reflect on after leaving this city again. Hopefully this is only the beginning. I want observations and questions to challenge me. And I want to face them head on, to confront them and grow as a person as a result.

I have so much left to learn. Can't I just be wise for my age? Alas, I have to suffer and struggle and stretch my mind and love and lose just like the rest of human life before I attain clarity and wisdom. And even then,

I may not obtain it…but it won't be for lack of trying!

AND SO, I said goodbye to who I'd been in Nashville. I said goodbye to Ryan, whose calls I would no longer receive. I said goodbye to using sex as a means to feel special. And though I still would have work to do before I was able to completely release the shame I felt regarding the court trial, I would take one step toward moving past the memory.

I went to visit the home I had lived in at the time of the crime. But the house was no longer there. Unable to rent it after my roommates and I moved out, the owner sold the property to someone in the music industry. The neighborhood was becoming home to a song-publishing district, so the buyer had the house moved to another location to make room for a high-rise complex. I drove by an empty lot. Now, several more years later, I bet the whole neighborhood would be unrecognizable to me. Someday I may go back and see for myself. But I don't have to, I've already said goodbye.

7
A French Fling

SOON AFTER RETURNING to Portland, I secured another part-time job to supplement my job at the Aladdin Theater. I began teaching English as a second language to adults at a local language academy. I'd had no teaching experience in the past, and I felt I was a terrible teacher. I loved engaging in cultural discussions with the advanced students, but I discovered how much work went into lesson planning and grading. Having been given no curriculum for any of my classes, I discovered I did not have the passion or drive to thoughtfully plan out daily activities and assignments that met the high expectations I placed on myself as a teacher. I committed to at least finishing out the fall term. Perhaps it would get easier with more experience.

I preferred to devote my energy to expanding upon my experience with men, however. Through new friends I'd made at the weekly blues dance I attended, I was invited to my first Portland house party. I'd seen one of the other guests, Jean-Luc, at lindy hop and blues events, but though he was physically attractive and had a name and an accent that conjured up all sorts of romantic imagery, I was not attracted to him—he seemed to have quite the ego. After talking a lot at the party, I realized he was actually rather humble. And he took a fancy to me. I was suddenly the envy of my coworkers. "Who is *he*?" they exclaimed when I had his social media profile open on my computer. I reveled in the goodness of it all.

I've been saying it to other people: your life can change so suddenly. Finally, it has happened to me. I went from the toughest couple of weeks in early August, then back to being myself and feeling so content and happy, now to feeling so unbelievably blessed and spoiled. Do I deserve to be this happy? Why have I been chosen? My life has shifted in less than a week. I have met the most amazing man…but the most incredible part is that he's attracted to me because I'm "smart, joyful, open-minded, and a pleasure to be around." He says I have an amazing personality. The unexpected part is that he has an amazing personality, is smart, kind, funny, athletic, and beautiful. How can a girl like me attract a guy like that? And HE pursued ME. And he's willing to wait for sex. Oh, and he's French. What?!

I find myself often questioning if this is really happening. Like, any day now, he will wake up and realize maybe I'm not as great as he thought…this has all been a mistake, and I will be left deeply hurt, but not surprised. And he will go on to be with multiple women because surely if he's into me, I must be just one of many, right? There couldn't possibly be qualities in myself that are unique and desirable on their own. My qualities are perhaps not only found but surpassed in multiple other women—more beautiful women. Women more comfortable and experienced with sex.

I know I should not have these thoughts. I know I have a lot to offer, but I feel this is a rare moment that someone else has recognized that. And to have that be someone so wonderful has left me in disbelief and wonder.

THE SENTENCES ***HE'S*** *willing to wait for sex* and *He's French* have no rightful place next to each other. I think we waited three nights.

I wasn't ready, but I went against my better judgment. It felt good to be desired. I was definitely attracted to him, but it was clear that an emotional connection was lacking—which is really what I was looking for. Once again, I fell into the pattern of attempting to use my body in order to feel loved. Quicksand is hard to climb out from.

He was honest from the start—he did not feel capable of falling in love. It was a feeling I could relate to, but I nonetheless did not want to hold back from trying. I was caught up in a fantasy again: girl falls for Frenchman, learns European flavor of making love, girl's sexual insecurities are healed, man falls in love for first time.

Though Latin Boris had made me suspect the French kiss had been misnamed, I discovered with Jean-Luc that the French could at least continue to vie for the title. But it felt like work reaching him on an emotional level. One night he arrived at my place late and crawled immediately into my bed. We had not seen each other in several days, and I was aching for emotional connection. I turned on the light to welcome him and inquire about his week, but he insisted we turn the lights off and instead get physical. My ego was bruised. I internalized that he preferred not to see me. *There must be something shameful about me,* I thought. Perhaps he wanted to fantasize I was someone else.

I was deeply hurt by my own self-degrading fantasy and lapsed into my role-playing persona of pretending I was enjoying sex. Yes, I enjoyed being touched, but emotionally I checked out and just wished the act would end so we could cuddle—and maybe even talk.

For about a month, we continued sneaking around, seeing each other when our schedules permitted. I say "sneaking around" because, well…things can get quite incestuous among dancers. Your friend's current boyfriend is your ex-boyfriend, who had an experimental stint with your other ex-boyfriend and so on. It was Jean-Luc's decision that we keep our relationship private, so as not to upset a recent former girlfriend of his who was a regular at dance events and parties.

I was okay with that decision initially. I enjoyed feeling a little naughty with my secret. However, before long I felt like perhaps he was hiding me because he was ashamed to be seen with me. I did not fully believe I was a sexual woman, or even girlfriend material. I still did not love myself or deem myself worthy.

The relationship reached the point where I felt that he would only prioritize seeing me if he assumed that he would get laid. I tested this by once texting him before his lunch break that I was horny. *Ding.* Immediate reply. He was on his way over. Upon his arrival, we engaged in some playful kissing, which I did so enjoy, but as he began to lift my shirt, I stopped him. Psych.

"I know you only have an hour break. That is not much time to engage in both sex and conversation, and I prefer conversation. Can we talk?"

Can we talk: the most mood killing line of all time. Queue faulty-recording-playback noise. His hands stopped in their tracks, my shirt falling back down to its proper position.

"Let's go to lunch," he replied. "We can take my car."

I was proud of myself for not simply responding to his expectation. I was going to speak my truth and stand up for myself.

He explained over lunch that his initial infatuation with me had worn off, as was his pattern in relationships. He would retreat into not feeling anything and simply respond to external physical stimuli. This scene had played out over and over again in his life, leaving a trail of broken hearts in his wake. He was scared he would never be able to fall in love. I felt empathy for him. His honesty was raw, his heart open. *This* was a man I wanted to know.

We took a short walk after lunch, and he asked me, "I know this sounds cliché, but I really mean it. I want to be friends with you. Will you consider being my friend?" I recognized a tangible trace of fear in his voice that I would say no. A rapid replay went through my mind, of being asked this same question by Ryan in Nashville. But I knew, wholeheartedly, this was different. My stomach didn't overturn at the suggestion. Yes, I wanted to be this man's friend.

A look of great relief replaced his apprehension as he hugged me.

And so he remains today, one of my closest friends. That was the Universe's plan all along, I suppose.

By early November I felt the urge to travel again. I'd met no one since Jean-Luc. I had received notice that I would be laid off from my teaching job mid-December (which I was actually glad about), and I knew that my position at the Aladdin Theater was one that would always be available to me. I had overnight petsitting jobs lined up through January, so embarking on my adventure at the end of that month seemed the perfect time.

Argentina was calling me back. Perhaps it was the comfort of the familiar streets and friends to fall back on. Or perhaps it was a desire to return to where I'd met Boris—the city seemed to hold promise in the realm of romance. At the very least, it was something to look forward to that would take my mind off heartbreak. I also concluded that if I committed to intensive Spanish classes while there, I'd be in a much better position to replace my part-time jobs with a consistent and meaningful career in international relations or other such field that might allow me to travel for a living.

I had a meager amount of savings, however, which I wasn't sure would last the three months I planned to spend in the country. I needed a cushion, and the Universe provided. Jean-Luc deeply believed in me and responded to what he could see was my spirit's intense calling by loaning me the money needed to ensure a safe journey. He insisted on helping me purchase travel insurance as well, offering me (and my parents) greater peace of mind.

But I had to wait three months before departing, a time period in which a lot can happen…

8
The Boy from New York City

DANCE HOUSE PARTIES were good luck for me. At the next one, I met a man with whom I instantly connected on an emotional level. From the beginning of the party, we were pretty much glued to a corner of the kitchen, engaged in conversation covering everything from our mutual desire to live abroad, our preference to travel rather than acquire possessions and "nest," and our passion for nature and the outdoors. He had moved to Portland from New York City to escape the mad pace and, well, his family. We clearly had a lot in common. We made plans to meet at a coffee shop later in the week to continue our discussion.

We spent nine hours at that coffee shop. Sam and I would spend several more evenings, and entire days, together over the next few weeks. It wasn't until just before I left to visit my family for Christmas that we made one of our outings an official date, however. We were both nervous to dive into a committed relationship—he had recently ended a shorter relationship, and I'd be leaving at the end of January for Argentina. Sam and I weren't sure how much we should get our hearts involved. A poem he wrote me said it beautifully:

To: Rebecca
From: Sam

> *I woke up with fear today*
> *fear of falling for you*
> *then you leaving*

for your next adventure
I see a lot of the nymph
in your soul
I'm being drawn into you
lured by your adventurous spirit
your openness
your progressiveness
your playfulness
your worldliness
your spiritual-ness
reminding me of my adventurous spirit
that I have put away for a short spell
trading it for some security
you are not like some women
who want to tame a man
coax him to settle down
I feel like those women
wanting to catch the nymph
to keep you
I know
only to quell the fear
fear of falling for you
you are easy to fall for
I dream of being invited
into your waterfall

I DID, INDEED, fear being tied down. But at this point in my life, a deeper fear was never being loved. We continued seeing each other, understanding that anything could happen while I was away. We'd see how our lives would unfold and how much we'd miss each other while apart.

I'd told Boris I was returning to Buenos Aires, and he met that information with great excitement and anticipation. He was, however, back together with his ex-girlfriend, and he knew I had just started seeing a man in Portland. We discussed at length various options for meeting up either in Buenos Aires or in Brazil, just as friends. But circumstances—mostly of the financial sort, we both claimed—would prevent the reunion from happening.

Maybe it was better this way. We had such different lives. Besides, I still had so much of myself left to discover.

> *This weekend was exhausting—both physically and emotionally. Sam and I went on a date Friday night. I had not seen him in a few days, and I was feeling very affectionate and connected to him. I was ready and wanting for his company and his touch. We came back to my place after going to the theater, and went right to bed. We began talking, and I felt ready to answer a question he had asked me over the phone the night before, regarding sex: "What do you like?"*
>
> *All discussions about sex lead me to fear, embarrassment, vulnerability, insecurity, and avoidance. This is the hardest subject for me to talk about. I fantasize in my mind ways to explain this to Sam…to answer his question. What it boils down to is lack of experience, and the intimidation and embarrassment that come along with that. I know having had sex with three men is more than enough to*

qualify as "experience," but what I'm embarrassed about is the kind of sex I've had—so simple, so routine, and so shut down on my behalf. I feel I know enough to give a man pleasure, but not enough to sustain his interest in a long-term relationship—nor to satisfy him with the degree of pleasure I am able to receive and express.

I think it would be best for me to just admit all of this before we have sex. And it is just so hard for me to say. It is so scary to think about admitting that I have never had an orgasm during sex—only by myself, and even that was a long time ago. I get moments of pleasure and desire from the act, but what I really can't wait for is for the man to orgasm, so it can end and he can hold me. Then I will have felt desired, and maybe even loved...sexy, like a woman.

So what do I like? I don't know. I like the feeling that comes afterward, and the rush leading up to the act...but I don't like the act itself. I am not comfortable releasing my soul, or even just my physical body, that way. I think what I need is the emotional attachment that comes with the physical—for the mental connection to be so powerful that it leads to physical culmination of emotional energy—that is the orgasm for me. And as of yet I have never felt that emotional climax. I've been too shut down.

So I was lying in bed with Sam, about to say all of that, when he admitted he was too tired to presently listen. I admire and respect his honesty, but I was feeling so open and vulnerable, only to have that barrier spring up. I immediately felt myself shut down emotionally, and I withdrew physically from his hold. Maybe it just wasn't the right time anyway…or maybe he's not the right person.

As much as I may be seeking emotional connection, I've noticed myself begin to emotionally detach from Sam, I think because I know I'm about to leave again. I feel so guilty when I feel myself withdrawing as a result of nothing anyone else has done…and even more ashamed when I act like nothing is wrong. But I am still open to seeing where this relationship leads. I suspect that being apart from each other will provide some clarity as to the possibility of creating something deeper together. We'll see if we miss each other.

I suppose I am fortunate that this trip to Argentina was already planned before we started dating, and not a result of my trying to escape my current demons again. I have to have faith that the trip will open my mind and my heart, and give me insight to my place in this world…and my place with another.

9
Notes from Buenos Aires

I LEFT PORTLAND for Buenos Aires. I arranged for my first month of housing with friends I had met on my previous trip, but left the remaining two months open in case I wanted to travel.

Jean-Luc gave me a journal just before my departure. Throughout the journal were famous quotes regarding traveling. He inscribed in the front cover, *My favorite quote is: "Life is either a daring adventure or nothing at all," by Helen Keller. I conclude your life is onto something worth writing down! —Jean-Luc*

I knew there was an important reason my soul was calling me to embark on this daring adventure, though I wasn't yet sure what it was. I spoke a lot with my soul over the next ninety days in Argentina, trying to discover what it had to teach me.

DAY 1

> *I can't believe I am back in Buenos Aires. It all seems so surreal; part of me feels like I'm simply recalling being here in my memory—that this is temporary, and I'll wake up back in Portland. Part of me feels also, that this is real—that I am a stranger in a strange land again. That I am alone, fearful of others trying to communicate with me. My stomach is all full of nerves...I am hungry but not wanting to shop in a foreign environment. I am lonely, but unable to talk to anyone. I am missing Sam, but unsure if that feeling*

comes from being alone and he is familiar, or just that, beautifully, I want him with me on my adventures.

I watched Into the Wild *on the plane last night, and the main character had secluded himself for so long, merely to realize right before his death that happiness didn't feel real to him unless it was shared with another. I am discovering that as well. Last time I was here, I had been so overstimulated for so long, that I relished the time alone and distance from everyone familiar. But I have had plenty of time now, since then…and now I desire a partner. And right now, I want that partner to be Sam.*

I could not believe it, but he told me he loves me on Friday night…my last night in Portland. He had been such a savior to me, helping me move and being my support, or my home base, as we like to call it. I feel so blessed to have him in my life. He's the first guy I've dated that I've told my parents about during the fact, and that has to mean something. I miss him already. He challenges me, and I believe I can learn a lot from him. I did not reply to his words with the same, but I don't think he expected me to. I feel like I have the ability to love him equally, I just think it takes me longer. I am hopeful that I will soon be able to return his sentiment, and I anticipate that day with humility and excitement.

DAY 11

A question has been nagging my mind since I arrived here in Buenos Aires: what am I doing here? I know I am meant to be here, but I have no idea as to why. Perhaps the impetus for the trip was that I was simply looking for an escape from my routine.

I have no desire to be back in Portland yet, but I'm still unsure if I came to the right place here. It's all so familiar, and I'm not able to explore myself and my surroundings in the way that I could before. Again, my emotions are intrinsically linked to my environment. If I'm not forced completely out of my comfort zone, and with no familiar faces, I fall into a comfortable, numb routine.

I'm not unhappy here. I wasn't unhappy in Portland. I've simply been numb…or maybe just "content," which to me is numb, as I crave feeling nothing but completely alive and aware. Instead, I've been unable to cry, to love, and even to hurt. I want to feel something. I haven't allowed myself to fall in love with others, because I'm afraid of attachment, and I've feared that I won't be loved in return. So I shut my emotions down, and I change my environment.

I am told I am courageous for traveling alone, for making things happen in my life, not just dreaming about them. But am I the weak one, escaping reality and emotions for "fresh starts"? Am I avoiding my fears, the same as those people who don't travel out of fear?

DAY 21

I can't believe I've only been here three weeks! When your environment, daily routine, social circle, and even language are flipped upside down overnight, it always feels like large expanses of time have gone by. I have had some significant changes in state of mind that I did not anticipate so early on. I have become bored with Buenos Aires. Not bored IN Buenos Aires, just bored with the city itself. It is constantly moving, but that constant motion is what in itself is boring. I have had to reanalyze my goals for this trip, as well as what is spiritually best for myself. I have reached stagnancy in this city in that regard. My spiritual world results from nature and consistent change of environment, and Buenos Aires can't offer me either. I read somewhere that in this city a view is rare and a sunset is priceless, and that really hit me…they're RIGHT! The "view" here is concrete structure after concrete structure, with no space in between. To see the sky, you have to look directly up, you cannot see it straight ahead. I am not inspired by that. I am delighted by the architecture and I recognize the glory of this city that once was, but I have determined that for myself to grow, I need peace. Nothingness. A view.

I have one more week of classes, then next Saturday I am taking a bus to Puerto Madryn for the week. It is the gateway to Peninsula Valdes off the southeast coast of Patagonia. After I return to Buenos Aires, I don't know where I will live or what I'll do…I'm working on some options that I'll write more about once they're arranged. I am certainly not ready to leave Argentina yet. I feel there's more to this country and more to this experience that I am capable of learning.

Day 27

I am on a bus to Puerto Madryn in Patagonia. My

heart is feeling heavy. I am aching to be with Sam. I received a package from him yesterday—so full of thought and care and love. It makes me feel so blessed to have found him—to have him love me! Suddenly this trip has become really hard. I have left the busy, distracting city of Buenos Aires. My classes have ended. I am left with no commitments, no home, no definite plans again. I normally thrive in this position of adventure and uncertainty, but instead I now feel empty. I have so many thoughts, so many jokes I want to share with Sam. I no longer want to be traveling alone.

I'm only 1/3 of the way along on this adventure…this adventure that is losing meaning, direction, and the thrill. I can't stop daydreaming about my future with Sam. I can't stop thinking about touching him. I am feeling pain, but I am welcoming it. I want to feel yearning for someone. I wanted this trip to answer some questions for me, and if I continue down this path, I believe it will.

DAY 32

This is my final night in Puerto Madryn before returning to Buenos Aires. I have decided I will then stay with a couple of different friends and enroll in Spanish classes again. It was nice to get out of the city for a week, and part of me will really miss this quiet coastal town. I love having my daily walks involve a view of the ocean. It's interesting to think that locals consistently pass by and don't make the effort to notice it, to take it in. Does everything of beauty lose its appeal when handed to you on a consistent basis? Maybe I'd rather treat myself to inconsistent doses of "soul food" in an effort to preserve its value.

I have enjoyed seeing another region of this vastly diverse country. Though Puerto Madryn is on the ocean, it is surrounded by desert. No trees are indigenous, only bush dots the landscape. Outside the town, however, is NOTHING. For as far as one can see, all that is visible is red dirt, sand, gravel, bush, and an occasional roadside shrine. Estancias, or ranches, operate portions of the land, true to gaucho lore. I really had the urge to hijack a horse and just ride the flatlands.

Though I greatly welcomed the ability to see beyond twenty feet around myself, witness a sunset, smell clean air, and feel the dirt beneath my feet, I still ached to see green vegetation—forests, moss, flowers. Though I took in the ocean with its saltwater smell and taste, blue canvas, and crashing waves, I still ached for nearby hiking trails, rolling hills, and rocky cliffs. I ached for Oregon.

I traveled all the way to the southernmost inhabited country, and you know what I'm realizing? Oregon already HAS much of what Argentina has to offer, and more. Mountains, ocean, desert, wineries, wildlife, a metropolitan city. All that separates us is a common language and culture.

DAY 41

Another week back in Buenos Aires, and my heart

still stings. For the first time in my life, I believe I am homesick. And not just for my country or culture, but for Portland. I believe I have found me a home! And, I am aching to be with someone in particular—I am homesick and missing someone! Really missing—feeling pain, fear, loneliness, emptiness…I had gone to travel and seek LIFE, and instead I found emptiness. It is of course an uncomfortable feeling, but also beautiful, a relief. I feel something! I have continuously asked God to challenge me, to make me feel alive, and he is answering my prayers.

I used to look at travel as my soul food. Now, I can't wait to go "home" and get my soul food…see the trees and mountains and green of Portland, to see Sam, to share my home and life in Portland with my parents when they visit in May. A friend of mine told me last week that she sensed I was in a dark place, and encouraged me not to feel pain from being away from Sam, that I should live each moment here to its fullest and experience the joy of being here and abroad. I told Sam this and how I felt so helpless to change how I feel, and he reminded me that I don't need to. That I shouldn't try to change it. I should revel in feeling something. This is what I asked for, right? Why do I always feel like I have to be joyful? Why does everyone else tell me I need to be? I am so thankful to finally feel understood, and loved for all my emotions. I am feeling these sad, lonely, empty emotions, and not trying to escape them. I am not trying to return home earlier. I am going to allow myself to remain in this uncomfortable place, so that I appreciate and recognize my "happy place" to its fullest. And so that I know I can survive difficult times.

DAY 53

I am ready to say goodbye to Buenos Aires again, at least for quite some time. It has left me not feeling defeated but rather empty. It is hard for me to imagine people being able to find inner peace in a city this size. Even any relaxation that may take place within a massage parlor, or a tai chi class, for example, must be depleted upon stepping back outside. It seems impossible to maintain a steady state of bliss. I think locals manage to find refuge within their homes, and among close familial and social relationships.

What I will miss about this city are its people. I have come to know so many beautiful souls during this journey. It is a shame that there are so many people in this world with whom we could form meaningful and powerful relationships, yet our paths will never cross, or we won't be placed in an environment that is conducive to deeper social and mental exploration. You could say that the Universe or God or another higher being controls who we cross paths with, so therefore we don't need to worry about initiating these relationships–those that are meant to happen, will. But as much as I believe in a higher influence, I find it impossible to believe that we aren't also all individually capable of seeking out environments that allow us to meet and connect with other "random" individuals. I think we have to accept a balance between the two theories. And in the meantime, I'll just go about my travels, and appreciate those connections and "random" gems I meet along the way.

So long, Buenos Aires.

10
The Center of Transformation

THE NEXT, and final, month in Argentina was the most significant. I met several gems, including my new God.

I had been in desperate need of open, green space and an environment in which to deeply explore my spirituality. I located a farm via the World Wide Organization of Organic Farmers—an online portal for connecting volunteers with farm projects that provide meals and lodging in exchange for service—in the tiny community of Capilla del Monte, set amid the sierras in the northern province of Córdoba. An Australian named Paul and a Venezuelan named Rosa owned the farm. They called it the Bliss Center. I was already in love.

They operated the center using only environmentally conscious and sustainable practices, and hosted educational sessions and treatments for natural healing, permaculture, and sustainability. They wanted to provide a space for people simply to share their bliss with others—be it dancing, poetry, yoga, art, or any other creative form of expression.

The center was accessed by walking the back streets of town, weaving into the valley. Along the way, one would pass thermal springs, a Zen Buddhist center, wild medicinal plants, as well as an abundance of wild food. There was no electricity from the grid, the water was pure, the air clear and dry, and the land untouched by any form of pollution. It sounded like the exact opposite of Buenos Aires. It was exactly what I needed.

Upon contacting Paul regarding volunteer opportunities, I was met with the reply that they were supposed to have been taken down from the WWOOF website; they weren't yet ready for volunteers. In fact, the Bliss Center was just a plot of empty land. The website depicted their vision for the center they would build, the gardens they would tend, and the community they would form—it was simply a tool to manifest their future endeavor. Nonetheless, I knew I needed to go there, and I needed to meet this couple. I persisted, offering my services regardless of them not being able to offer me accommodation. Paul replied to my insistence with a congratulatory, "I like your style." They welcomed my enthusiasm and perseverance, and I welcomed their willingness to share their wisdom and passion.

A ten-hour overnight bus ride from Buenos Aires brought me to the capital city of Córdoba, where I boarded a two-and-a-half-hour bus to Capilla del Monte. At my stop I lugged my backpack on yet again and set about finding a hostel. It was the day after Easter weekend, and most guest accommodations were about to close for the season. I found one hostel open for one more night. I checked in and took a nap. I'd worry about tomorrow when it got here.

A few hours later, feeling somewhat refreshed, I shared Paul and Rosa's address with the hostel owner. She looked inquisitively at the street name. Hmm, well, it was a small town… I mentioned that it was the home of Paul and Rosa.

"Ahhh!!! *La casa de Paulo y Rosa*!!!" They may not have a farm yet, but they clearly were part of a bigger community.

She offered me detailed directions on how to arrive by foot. I left my backpack in the hostel locker and took in the beautiful walk through the residential part of town: gravel and dirt paths, with the occasional cow, horse, or chicken crossing the path. I'd later learn the commercial part of town consisted of one paved road lined with charming spiritual and metaphysical book and gem shops, artisan craft and culinary shops, and a few restaurants and natural food stores.

I felt as at home in the town as I did at Paul and Rosa's—they welcomed me warmly, with such pure, divine energy. After my long journey, I felt relief to be around people who not only spoke my vernacular but also my spiritual language. Their home was beautifully decorated and furnished with locally made crafts; the floors and walls were tiled in an array of colors; an orange and red linen with the om symbol hung above the living room couch. The best feature was the view. A large window overlooked the undeveloped valley beyond, with Mount Uritorco standing like a beacon in the distance. I'd read about this mountain: it was the site of several UFO sightings and other mysterious phenomena—members of NASA had been here many times to study these strange occurrences—and Paul and Rosa had a front-row view. They invited me to join them for dinner and a community dance performance in town. As I sat next to Rosa that night, her inner glow was contagious. I knew the following month held great promise for my personal journey. I couldn't wait to experience the ride.

The following week, with the hostel closed, I stayed at a hotel—which would soon close as well. I spent two entire days in bed with food poisoning. Paul and Rosa were both natural healers—Paul was a polarity therapist and breath worker, and Rosa practiced reiki—and it was during Paul's work on me while I was physically ill that he brought to my attention that there was a significant energetic disconnect between my body's upper and lower halves. "It's as if your body has been divided; your energy does not flow freely through," he shared. *Hmm…interesting.*

Once I recovered from my illness, Paul used his connections to arrange extremely affordable housing for me in a friend's guest *cabaña,* normally used to host visiting family and friends. It was a true gift sent to me from the Universe, a private sanctuary with a view of the nearby sierras and neighboring farms. The two-bedroom unit, with a full bathroom and kitchen, was in actuality too big for just one person. I invited a new friend I'd met through Paul and Rosa, who was having a challenging time finding an affordable place, to move in with me for the remaining three weeks of my stay.

Lisa, a traveler from Sweden, would become a beautiful, supportive presence for me during my journey. We were both spiritual seekers, hoping to be inspired by the transformative energy of this magical oasis in northern Argentina. Capilla del Monte is known as one of the world's energy centers; it was the Center of

Transformation. One of my favorite memories from my time in Capilla was waking up each morning and preparing tea to the sound of Lisa on the front porch chanting *om* during her daily yoga and meditation practice. Though I hadn't yet begun my own practice, the divine energy I could feel emanating from her being as she practiced would later inspire me to begin.

My Capilla spiritual practice started with a series of books Paul and Rosa loaned me, Conversations with God, by Neale Donald Walsch. I know now that there are a great number of books that share the same message, but these particular books spoke to me in a manner that I was most open to receiving at the time. The author lived in southern Oregon and was originally from Milwaukee, Wisconsin—where I was born. This example reinforced the lesson I was finally learning—that you often have to move on to see what you had available to you all along. It took traveling all the way to Argentina to discover the books that would change my life forever.

I was intrigued from the first page. Raised in a Christian home, I knew there were certain guidelines (i.e., strict commandments) that a proper Christian was to follow or else there would be consequences (i.e., eternal damnation in hell). Within these commandments, I was to make no comparison between God and myself; God was separate from me, higher than me, holier than me.

Along came this book—which the author described as having been dictated through God—that claimed that God is not separate from me at all. Rather, I am one *with* God; since we are one, there is no hierarchy between us.

What's more, God has no rules or requirements. God wants and needs nothing, demands and commands nothing. There is no right, and no wrong, in this God's eyes. *Hallelujah! Now this is a God worth getting to know!* I thought. I fell in love with him—or her, as this God is genderless.

All that matters to *this* God is that each of us follow our own soul's purpose in life, and that purpose dictates whether what we do is "right" or "wrong," in relation to where we—our souls—want to go. Instead of right or wrong, there is only "what works" and "what doesn't work," given what it is that we are trying to do. There is no such thing as an absolute or objective truth but rather only our own subjective, personal truth. And with no absolute truth about what is right or wrong, there is no opportunity to condemn a person to hell—in fact, this belief system is based on the concept that there *is* no such place as hell, merely the hell on earth we create within our own minds.

These concepts stirred things up for me, to put it lightly. Suddenly, I felt cheated. You mean all of those threats about God condemning my soul for having sex outside of marriage were simply not true?! In fact, the book suggests that marriage itself was constructed not by God but by man and religion as a contract—an artificial construction—designed to govern each other's behavior and create a false impression of security, or "foreverness" in a temporary world.

It goes on to propose that marriage laws violate the natural law that love is unlimited, eternal, and free.

Rather than being an announcement of love, marriage (as we have traditionally constructed it) is, therefore, really an announcement of fear. These laws are an attempt to guarantee that what is now will *always* be—something that we can never guarantee. Instead, we are not to expect or even hope that what we think we need in life will be supplied by another but rather to know that everything we need in life resides *within* us. Relationships should serve to inspire us and provide us the opportunity to strive toward being the best version of ourselves we can be.

These concepts resonated so deeply in my soul that I knew they were my personal truth—and had always been. But as the book explained by using the concept of the law of opposites, the moment we declare who we are, what we want, or where we are going, the Universe steps in to offer us the *opposite* of that which we declare. For without a context within which to experience a contrast, we cannot know ourselves to be, do, or have anything. So, when I wished to experience myself as love, its opposite—fear—stepped in, in the form of anger and resentment. How dare my church, my teachers, and my family sell me such...*bullshit* all my life?

I began to recall and analyze all the teachings of my youth and guidelines that had constructed my life, and I was furious. And unfortunately, I took it out on the people dearest to me. Instead of practicing this new way of being in the way it was meant to be practiced, I isolated myself from those back home who did not agree with me. I wrote hurtful e-mails, expressing why I didn't want to attend my brother's upcoming traditional Christian wedding. I was so disgusted with the institution of marriage and its connection to the Bible that I just couldn't imagine sitting in the church, witnessing vows that I perceived to place constraint and limits on the spirit. My family reacted to my antics with surprise but not with judgment—by now they were getting used to me having a nontraditional lifestyle and somewhat "radical" ideas.

Though I didn't realize it at the time, I loved my brother so much that I knew it would be painful for me to feign support of what I deemed his demise. But instead of explaining what I was feeling with love, I expressed it with anger and judgment. How could he be so…ignorant?

How could I be so horrible? Now, I've passed through that place of opposition and truly understand that there is no absolute "right" or "wrong," except in the context of my own highest self's announcement of my own truth. I know it was not my highest self that expressed my opinion in the way that I did, nor was it my place to make the judgment that this form of marriage was "wrong" for my brother. I am deeply regretful. But do you know what? My brother, and my parents, loved me anyway. What a lesson in love and the true meaning of divinity.

This exposure to these spiritual concepts planted the seed for the belief system by which I would later seek to live each moment of my life. But my time in Capilla was filled with confusion and the processing of a complexity of emotions. It was also filled with great peace. I developed a daily routine of enjoying breakfast and spiritual discussion with Lisa, followed by a solo walk along the river, where I would sit for hours, reading and journaling, writing down questions from the books that I couldn't quite grasp. It's not an easy process, to decondition one's brain and body after years of thinking and living a certain way. I dove in headfirst, but it would take years to fully integrate. (Well, let's face it, I'm still integrating it all, and likely will be the rest of my life.)

In addition to my own solo exploration of the town and myself, I enjoyed many shared adventures with my new friends. Among my favorite was an all-day horseback ride with a true gaucho for a guide. It was on this ride that I ate my very first fig. I had no idea what I'd been missing. I'd initially denied the offer from my guide—I was not a fan of Fig Newtons growing up, as they were the consolation prize in my family when real dessert, chocolate, was not around. After hearing the rest of the group rave about these wild mountain figs, I broke down. Bliss. Absolute bliss. I now have become an expert in where to find "wild" fig trees in Portland. I'm the first to arrive at the local park with my bags ready to fill with fig after glorious fig each fall. I suspect that the "forbidden fruit" the Bible speaks of was actually the fig. If we're going to condemn pleasure, that would be where I would start.

I also went on various hikes in the area; I climbed Mount Uritorco with Rosa and Los Terrones with Lisa. Just outside of town, Los Terrones, consisted of a collection of sacred ground formations, including one called the Finger of God, pointing toward the heavens. I felt

God's presence all around me. At the peak of one sierra, someone had hung a large quartz crystal for wanderers to stand beneath and take in the magical energy of the region.

Paul's birthday took place during my visit, and to celebrate, a small group of us hiked to what would be the Bliss Center plot and enjoyed a picnic together. People brought musical instruments, and before long everyone was up dancing. But this wasn't the kind of dancing I was used to. This was my first exposure to ecstatic dancing, and it was a sight to behold. At one point, a friend grabbed a roll of toilet paper (it occurs to me now as quite thoughtful to have brought a roll of toilet paper on our excursion) and began dancing with it…that is, unrolling it, throwing it, circling within it. I laughed with delight. These people knew how to have a good time! Despite my enjoyment of their spectacle, I was hesitant to join in. I was still uncomfortable using my body for self-expression; I know it sounds contradictory, as I was an avid blues and swing dancer even at that time, but the distinction was that I practiced partner dancing. I was not yet comfortable being "out there" alone, letting go of my *own* spirit.

One of my final memories from my time in Capilla was when Rosa, a female friend of hers, and I decided to go for a swim in the river. We walked quite a ways from town and were in a relatively secluded spot. Rosa and her friend decided to swim naked and invited me to join them. I was too shy and uncomfortable with my own nudity to participate, but I admired their courage and comfort with their own bodies. It wasn't long before the local *policía* got wind of their adventure and came over to investigate. I think he just wanted a closer look at the little escapade, but he insisted there were children farther downriver whose parents were offended. We all lamented how sad the state of our society was, that going for a swim in nature in our most natural state was deemed offensive. It doesn't have to be that way.

And with that memory, my four weeks in Capilla, and therefore my three months in Argentina, came to a bittersweet end. Along with the end of my trip came the end of my journaling. I returned to Portland and entered into what I consider my first "real" relationship. I suppose I felt I no longer needed a journal with which to share my deepest thoughts—I now had a partner in life. By the end of my trip, I believed I was ready to return Sam's love. I couldn't wait to return to Portland to express this newfound sentiment in person. And I did, my first night back—at the same restaurant we had eaten at my last night in Portland, when he'd told me he loved me. Soon afterward, I moved in with Sam. And there I would spend the next five years of my life, exploring myself.

II
Exploring Myself

11
Trouble in Bed

I RETURNED TO Portland full of idealistic optimism. I had just discovered *so* much. I had filled a thick notebook with quote after quote from the spirituality books I'd read that I wanted to share with Sam and discuss in-depth. I could not wait to further explore these concepts with a partner—and by doing so explore partnership in and of itself.

While apart, Sam and I had compiled an extensive list of activities. There was so much we wanted to experience together, as if we'd both been waiting a lifetime for the chance to truly live. First on our list was a camping trip to eastern Oregon. It was still early in the season, but the high desert climate provided enough warmth for a comfortable weekend excursion. Not that we need have worried—I learned then that Sam was an avid survival enthusiast, to put it lightly. We had emergency blankets, hand warmers, and layer upon layer of thermal clothing; this detailed planning was a scene that would play out before every camping excursion for the next five years and would spark a friendly competition between my father, who fancied himself an outdoors expert, and Sam.

The landscape of the region reminded me so significantly of both the Patagonian desert and the northern sierras of Argentina. I realized again that one need not travel so far to experience breathtaking beauty—and that there are striking similarities in landscape even thousands of miles apart. I was so grateful and glad to be back in Oregon, and back with Sam, but I again felt like I had this alternate travel life that the Oregon rain would wash away.

I fought to continue my spiritual path; I use the word *fought* because the trappings of the world kept trying to stand stubbornly in my way. Not only did I have to once again begin a job hunt—or at least figure out how to supplement my part-time work at the Aladdin Theater—I also had to figure out my living situation. My personal time was limited, and my social time was not what I'd become accustomed to in Capilla del Monte. Not everyone in my life in Portland wanted to engage with me in deep spiritual conversation and personal growth. Actually, no one did.

Sam had dabbled in martial arts in the past, so I knew that some of these concepts were already available to him. I assumed that he wanted to observe and analyze all aspects of life within that lens—all the time. He didn't. About halfway through the second day of the camping trip, he paused during our hike to move a worm from the middle of the trail.

"That's really sweet of you," I began, "but what if that worm's journey required being in harm's way? What if it was in the exact right place at the right time, in order to know and experience its soul's purpose?"

"Stop! Just stop, please!"

I could have laughed, because truly it was funny. But instead I chose to be hurt and judgmental. I already started questioning the feasibility of our relationship; would he be able to keep up with me spiritually? This pattern would carry on for the next several years of partnership. At the slightest disagreement, my mind would project, *Is this going to work? Does he have what I need in a partner?* I would later learn that these thoughts are like poison; there is overt toxicity in responding to challenges with internal threats and an all-or-nothing mentality. Of course, such questions *should* be asked pertaining to larger life choices and questions of compatibility but perhaps not every time one's partner leaves a spoon in the sink.

We may have lacked spiritual connection within our relationship, but we were incredibly compatible as roommates, travel companions, and best friends. These characteristics made it possible for us to want to brush off the biggest detriment to the sustainability of our relationship. Sex was a major struggle for us. We explored every possible factor outside of our physical connection with the hope that we'd hit gold: "Aha! *That* is the problem! Smooth sailing from here on out!"

Of course, the pendulum swung to me as the one needing to do some serious work around the sex issue. I had admitted that I'd experienced a lifetime of sexual shame and fear and had never experienced an orgasm with a partner. I was the one who never wanted to initiate sex, who energetically blocked advances, and who basically wanted sex to be over with just as soon as it began. Avoiding sex meant avoiding feeling like a fraud. Though I wanted to believe that relationships didn't have to consist of a normal sex life (after all, what is *normal*?), I could not deny that something was askew. I knew I needed to come to peace with sex, and my own sexuality. Armed with my travel and life experiences, my journaling and informal studying, and my dancing, I had the tools (not just the longing or awareness) to make the change.

One of my favorite movies is *The Peaceful Warrior,* based on the book *Way of the Peaceful Warrior,* by Dan Millman. My favorite scene is when the main character, Dan's younger self, has a dream in which he is standing at the top of a clock tower on the UC Berkeley campus. He climbed to the top to consider jumping off, but once there he encounters another student considering the same critical attempt. Dan tries to talk the other student out of jumping, but the student's ego, his back turned to Dan, needs to demonstrate his fearlessness. When he finally turns, Dan is shocked to discover that the other student is…himself. His old self, taunting him. He has the choice to save this other man or let him go. When the old self realizes that Dan is seriously considering letting him go, he begins to panic. The most powerful moment is when the character begins to cry, screaming, "Do you *know* who you *are,* without *me*?"

I return to this scene in my mind countless times. We are repeatedly offered this decision throughout our lives. Are we willing to take the risk? Are we brave enough to let go of the only version of ourselves that we conceptually *know* and embrace the uncertainty that comes with knowing ourselves in a deeper, more meaningful, more authentic way?

It can be scary. It can feel like jumping off a cliff, into an abyss. But it can also be so incredibly worth it.

12
Breaking Fertile Ground

I STOPPED TAKING the birth control pill.

It was a huge choice, one worthy of its own line. I had long believed that our bodies are not meant to take hormones on such a consistent basis—it had been ten years straight that I'd been on the pill, simply in an effort to have a period. I knew I needed to get to know my body in its most natural state. If I continued to stay on the pill, I would continue to mask an underlying issue that had not yet been revealed. Irregularities or discomfort in our bodies are meant as warning signs that there's something larger we need to pay attention to. If we mask those symptoms, we mask our body's wisdom.

Without the pill to regulate it, my period, when it did irregularly show up, would last up to two weeks and be accompanied with the worst cramps I'd ever experienced. I finally went to see a doctor. She recommended an ultrasound, which showed that I had a condition called PCOS (polycystic ovarian syndrome). Guess what the recommended treatment was for the condition. The birth control pill.

I fought the urge to panic. I left with the results of my blood test and ultrasound, which had been described to me with next to no detail and returned home to do some serious Googling, a step my doctor had recommended. I won't grapple too deeply with this concept here, but I will say I find it a sad statement on our health care system that people often feel forced to rely more on Google than doctors.

Though I found an abundance of information about PCOS on the internet, I found much more value within Christiane Northrup's *Women's Bodies, Women's Wisdom,* which a friend who worked in the healthcare field recommended to me. A greater gem for that time of my life could not have been found. I learned that these cysts are actually underdeveloped eggs; my body was not even ovulating. Northrup described the resulting disorder as extremely complex due to its deep connection to a woman's emotions, diet, personal history, and beliefs about herself. Northrup wrote that negative feelings about being female, as well as feelings of subordination or inferiority, can create stresses in the body that manifest in the suppression of ovarian and menstrual cycle functioning. This process is, in essence, an attempt to prevent becoming a fully mature woman.

This realization blew me away. I did feel inferior to other women who had active sex lives; subconsciously, I'd wanted to stay a girl—or a tomboy—to avoid the embarrassment that I felt would inevitably come when my lack of sexual experience was revealed. I so badly wanted to be a woman, but I dreaded what I had to do to get there in equal proportion. Later, as a result of continued spiritual study, I came to believe that our society commonly operates on a have-do-be paradigm but that life functions within a be-do-have paradigm. For example, I had been conditioned to think that I had to have things in order to do things so that I can be what I want to be. I had it backward. I now believe that the quickest path to ecstasy is to master the practice of being what I wish to be first. If I *be*lieved I was already a woman, I would *do*…well, a man…and, umm, *have* an orgasm. Okay, let me offer a better example.

Let's say I wish to be happy as my end result. If I make the choice to start even just one day with a smile and the *be*lief that I am happy, perhaps I would greet others with more enthusiasm at work or at the checkout counter. I might tip a little extra at lunch or give a compliment to a coworker. Since positive energy attracts more positive energy, I will inevitably "have" happiness. It will be offered to me simply as a result of doing what it is that my state of being leads me to do. I have found this to be a powerful practice.

I realized after reading Northrup's interpretation of possible causes of PCOS that I had internalized over the years that women are inferior to men. It could have come from years of wanting what I believed my brother had: more freedom, a bigger voice, even simply more physical strength. I had struggled, for example, with men opening car doors for me. I felt it was an indication that I was weaker. I always wanted to be treated as one of the guys—guys were stronger and more confident; they "accomplished" so much more, I thought.

Instead of claiming this physical "disorder" as part of my identity and as a lifelong condition, I followed Northrup's advice to try to make peace with my femininity and sexuality. I now recognized the inner battle at play, between my innate nature as a woman and my ingrained belief that I wasn't *already* a woman—and also my belief that men were superior to women. I implemented my new personal goals to read literature that celebrated the feminine spirit, to watch more movies with strong female leads, and for the first time in my adult life, to form solid bonds with other women. I also sought support from professionals.

I started seeing a naturopathic doctor—one who had PCOS herself. She gave me a much more detailed account of what the condition entailed and a breakdown of how my particular body displayed some, but fortunately not all, of its symptoms. She recommended dietary changes, and I started getting massages and energy work done; it was through this experience that I again was told that my upper body seemed cut off from my lower body.

"Take a deep breath," I was instructed.

I inhaled. The therapist waited.

"Take a deep breath," she repeated.

I again inhaled.

"No, from *here*, a real, actual breath." She placed her hand on my abdomen.

Oh, wow. I'm supposed to breathe from there? I thought. All my life (for all I know), I'd only been taking partial breaths. I've since learned that most adults have to relearn how to breathe properly—as babies we breathe from the gut, but somewhere along the line, we move to breathing shallowly, from the chest—and I was no exception.

I also joined a women's therapy group called How's Your Sex Life? Eight weeks of sitting in a circle with other women, discussing our sexual problems. It was a wide spectrum of women—married, divorced, never married, straight, gay, bisexual—but we were all there for the same reason. Sex was *hard*. I was terrified to speak up those first couple of weeks. I had not told many people—not even all of my sexual partners—that I had never experienced orgasm with a partner. We went around the circle and were encouraged to share as much of our story and reason for being there as we felt comfortable sharing. I knew that for me to get the greatest benefit from the group, I had to say it.

"Hello, my name is Rebecca, and I've never had an orgasm."

My heart was racing, and my mouth was dry. But I said it. And do you know what? No one looked at me funny. No one even flinched. And from that point on, talking about sex was so much easier. After eight weeks of discussing everything from desire, seduction, sexual shame, fear, power—and yes, orgasm—I felt there was nothing I couldn't say anymore. At least not within this group of women.

I couldn't get enough. I joined three more groups with more specific focuses. Each group consisted of about ten women—all different ages, professions, and sexual histories. I looked around the room at all these beautiful women. It struck me that if I had been introduced to any of them at a party, or worked with them, or had seen any of them walking down the street, I would have never assumed that they didn't have active, thriving sex lives. *Oh, the assumptions we make*, I thought. These groups were a huge turning point for me. I had felt so alone on my journey toward accepting myself as a sexual being and had carried all of this shame inside of me. Now, I had a safe place to practice its release. And by all of us practicing using the same voice of transparency and vulnerability, we found that we were not alone—but rather, were *all one*. So often we focus on our differences, but what if we focus on our similarities? Aren't we all struggling to figure out this whole "human experience" thing?

Another transformative lesson I gained from the women's groups was the redefinition of the word *vulnerable*. My earliest association with the word was my annual pelvic exam, which for me was at the age of sixteen rather than the customary age of eighteen. To expose the most private part of myself to a near stranger, who would not only just look "down there" but stick her fingers inside was beyond what I could emotionally handle. How I got through it, I don't know. I quite literally wanted to die. After being warned about the dangers of toxic shock syndrome in middle school, I wouldn't even let a tampon up in there.

Each visit, I experienced the same scenario. As I lay undressed and splayed, the doctor would ask me to spread my legs "wider, please…even wider" before inserting the metal forceps. After poking around in there for a bit, she'd pull the tool out and say, "I forgot how long your vaginal canal is. I'll have to get the extra-long forceps from the back—excuse me for a minute." She'd leave me there to literally hang out. A moment later I'd hear her call loudly down the hall, "Marge? Can you get me the giant forceps? I've got a special patient here." She'd return a minute later, forceps in hand, and apologize that they weren't warmed up like the other pair, as this size was rarely used. Year after year, this scene played out. And year after year, I was mortified. And therefore, I considered the word *vulnerable* to be a synonym for *hell*.

So when the theme of one week of my women's group was announced to be Embracing Vulnerability, I desperately wanted to go home "sick." *Oh* hell *no*, I thought. *I'm not embracing that shit.* But I stayed. And though it didn't happen overnight, I learned that embracing vulnerability is a necessary path to experiencing ecstasy. It's only by putting ourselves out there, truthfully and completely, that we can experience the highest emotions available in the human experience. I had numbed my emotions over the years, preferring to stay in a steady, comfortable place. It hurt less. But, I discovered, it also kept me from experiencing extreme joy.

A general perception is that exposing our vulnerability—our fears, our inadequacies, our limitations—makes us appear weak. In reality, it takes greater inner strength to admit our fears than to keep them hidden. When we allow ourselves to be vulnerable, we open ourselves up to receive the gifts that flow from the deepest nature of humanity—compassion, forgiveness, generosity, support, and love. Often, we hold back from exposing the most intimate parts of ourselves because we aren't familiar with the most intimate parts of another. It takes great courage to break through this barrier that may exist in our relationships and stand strongly while declaring, "I'll go first."

When we do go first, a heavy burden lifts not just from our own shoulders but most likely from the shoulders of the person we opened up to. I've often found myself hearing, "I've never told anyone else this, but..." as a safe space is created for friends or lovers to embrace their own vulnerability, and perhaps release their own shame. Our own vulnerability hence becomes a beautiful gift to another.

One of the places embracing vulnerability can have the biggest impact is in the bedroom. Through my women's group, I learned that it is okay to ask for what I need. Whether it is to be touched in a certain way, in a certain place, for a certain duration...or even to say *no* when I really didn't want to be touched at all, there is no need to feel embarrassed or ashamed. Yes, I may risk feeling hurt or disappointed by my partner's response, but a greater risk is never getting what I really want. And I may discover that my current partner isn't actually capable of giving what I want. Again, that can be an extremely scary realization, but at least knowing that puts me in a position to make better choices, more aligned with my own soul. And soul choices always lead to greater happiness in the end.

13
Homework

THE THERAPY GROUPS weren't all in-session work—we also had homework. The kind of homework that most people indulge in without having to be told to do. I, however, dreaded my homework. I had always been such a diligent student that I went for extra credit every chance I could. And here I was questioning my therapist: "Really, Ms. Johnson? Do I *have* to?"

I had to masturbate.

I had privately indulged in the practice as an innocent child, but as an adult I had grown to completely ignore that the opportunity existed. It seemed like a waste of time. I'd rather be soaking in a warm bath, reading a good book. Eating chocolate. Working on my connection with a partner who wasn't me. But now, I had carefully laid out instructions to explore myself, using various techniques and...toys. I had to go shopping. I gathered the courage to walk in to one of the feminist sex shops in the city, head held high, and administer a cheerful hello to the staff, role-playing a sex-positive woman that had been there many times.

"Excuse me, would you like to see a demonstration of the new Rabbit Habit Vibrator?"

"Oh, who, me?" I looked around nervously.

"Yes, it has variable speeds and a cordless base with rotating pearls in a squared-off soft casing."

For a moment I wasn't sure I'd walked into the right store. Could this be an annex of a power-tool store next door? I quickly glanced around the room at the displays of phallic "tools." No, I was in the right place.

"Oh, no, thank you. It will just be a quick in-and-out for me." I cringed as I realized my poor choice of words for this particular shopping experience.

"Well, let me know if I can help you find anything. We have some new strap-on collars and some locally made feather ticklers near the checkout counter."

Of course you do...how Portland of you, I thought, amused. Despite my best efforts to act natural, I flashed an uncomfortable smile and replied, "Thank you," and made my way over to the literary section.

In addition to toys, I had been instructed to buy two books—one that resonated with me as something I had a genuine interest in and another that caused me to step far outside of my comfort zone to buy. I bought a book on tantric sex that seemed more like spiritual reading, and a photo book on bondage that would likely answer questions I didn't even know I had.

For the toys portion of my homework, I settled on the FingO, a mini vibrator on a ring—easy to hide inside a purse, should one need access to a pick-me-up at any time of day. I was told by the salesclerk they were quite convenient while driving—and that being stopped at a red light would never be more fun. A bigger investment was a stainless-steel kegel exerciser (which could double as a dildo). Throw in a bottle of Sliquid, and I figured I was all set for a night of serious study.

I was to gradually ease into this new world of self-pleasure. I checked out *The Passion Prescription* by Laura

Berman from the library, which includes a wonderful outline for a ten-week progression for the aspiring empress of sex and masturbation. Week one began with an anatomy lesson. I had never even really looked *down there.* Even when washing myself, I did so with my eyes averted. *Good girls don't look down there,* I still thought. Mirror in hand, I explored the layers and textures I had not yet become familiar with and compared them with the diagram in the book. I was somewhat bored, and somewhat fascinated with what I found. I remembered something about this in sex ed class in the fourth and sixth grades. Our homework at the time, however, certainly didn't encourage us to apply what we learned to our own bodies.

I braced myself for week two: masturbate at least once. *What a drag,* I thought. *This will be a waste of time.* But I committed to following the steps. I reached for my FingO and began to tease myself. It felt...nice. I fought the urge to consider a minute or two sufficient practice, and I allowed myself a good twenty minutes of exploration before declaring, "All right, glad *that's* over with."

Reporting back to my women's group later in the week, I proudly stated that I had completed my homework. Naturally, they were curious how the experience went for me, and when I shared that it was simply "okay," I was met with further questioning as to what particular toys I'd used. My response was followed by everyone's exclamation that I needed something more intense. The Magic Wand and Betty Dodson's video *Celebrating Orgasm.* Now *that* was an experience. The video showcases five different women as Betty led them to orgasm during private, hands-on coaching sessions. All of them used the Magic Wand.

Thus began my extensive research into the realm of self-love. I explored Dodson's work, including her classic, *Sex for One*, and *Viva la Vulva* and Julia Heiman's *Becoming Orgasmic*, all the while practicing with new toys and techniques. (By the way, the Magic Wand is a powerful thing.) All of these resources led me to accept and appreciate my sexuality and helped to normalize the act of self-love. I was able to reach orgasm by myself before long, though it would take years to truly let myself go and experience a deeper energetic release with a partner. Like all things, sex requires practice, and I believe my experience will continue to get better and better.

As I became more comfortable with my body and with expressing my sexuality, I decided to do something special to celebrate my twenty-eighth birthday. I had professional semi-nude photos taken. I found a local photographer who specialized in boudoir photography. Her art was inspired by the desire to empower women to embrace their bodies and their sexuality—exactly what I was looking for. Even preparing for the photo shoot was a growth opportunity for me. For the first time in my life, I allowed myself to spend significant money on fancy lingerie and accessories. I finally felt that I deserved it.

When I received the photos back, I had to admit I was proud of them. I created a collage, accenting the photos with favorite cutouts of '50s pinups—mostly women joyously naked amid nature—and conspicuously displayed on the wall by my side of the bed, so that each morning when I woke up, it was the first thing I saw. It was a reminder to start my day with the affirmation that I was a sexy, confident, beautiful woman. And there was no shame in that.

I took advantage of another opportunity to celebrate nudity when one of the women in my therapy group invited us to see her perform in an amateur burlesque show. She would work through her own sexual fears by choreographing and performing a playful striptease as part of the culmination of an eight-week workshop. She would bare all for a crowd of encouraging supporters. How brave those women were; I was so proud of them all. She inspired me to dabble in burlesque dancing myself. The modern lindy hop scene had begun to incorporate burlesque movements into its repertoire, so the dance was not as foreign to me as it once had been. I'd always admired the women who elected to take the burlesque class options at lindy hop workshops. I hadn't felt comfortable participating in them before—the students were not only learning seductive moves but were doing them alone, without a dance partner to hide behind, and in front of giant mirrors. I was proud of myself for stepping outside my comfort zone to practice seductive solo moves in class—even if we all remained clothed and without an audience.

It was at this time, amid all of these shifts in my beliefs about sex and my relationship to it, that some physical changes began to happen within my body. My period started coming regularly. I had never reverted to birth control pills, as my Western doctor had advised. I instead started tracking my cycle, using the methods described in Toni Weschler's book, *Taking Charge of Your Fertility*. With daily tracking of my basal body temperature, cervical fluid pattern, and cervical position, I accurately predicted days of ovulation, and therefore menstruation. I believe that even this simple awareness of and appreciation for how my body works created a safe space for my body to perform its natural functions. Now that I was ovulating regularly, the ovarian cysts disappeared on their own.

I learned that we have way more control over our own fertility than the medical industry and the media would have us believe. It's sad, but true, that there lies much more profit in having us believe we need to spend thousands of dollars on birth control pills, IUDs, vasectomies, and various methods of artificial insemination. Western medicine does have its place, but it's a shame that it's not customary to be told of the strength of alternative options.

I came to appreciate the power I have over my own body, as well as the grandeur of the female body; we are designed to function so intricately and exquisitely—and no one had ever told me.

14
Partner Practice

DESPITE ALL THE progress I made via my self-exploration and practice, I knew that what I was learning also had to be applied to my partnership. Sam and I engaged in survey after survey to cerebrally wrap our brains around our problems with desire. We attended a couple's workshop on compassionate communication, to better support the sharing of our individual preferences and challenges. We started taking yoga together to harvest a deeper spiritual connection between us. We read John Gottman's *The Seven Principles for Making Marriage Work*—a highly impactful book not just for legally married couples—which brought to light many of our destructive behavioral patterns. We followed homework from my therapist, taking turns touching various parts of each other's body and rating each type and area of touch to reveal our physical preferences.

Each of these activities brought us closer together emotionally. Our partnership became quite solid in the realm of communication and companionship. But there we were again—excellent companions. We loved each other dearly, but we weren't drawn to each other sexually. All of the rose petals sprinkled on the bed and the chocolate and the wine in the world could not make up for the lack of sexual chemistry we felt when together.

Bless our hearts, we tried.

Sam bought me new toys to try, sexy lingerie and feminine jewelry, dresses and shoes, and manicures and pedicures. Sometimes the pampering and showiness helped, but mostly it didn't. The chemistry just wasn't there.

I was resistant, for a long time, to Sam's gifts. I thought at first that he was trying to make me into something I wasn't. If he couldn't accept my appearance as it was, could he ever really accept me? I eventually got over that fear and realized the heart of his efforts. They were attempts to keep us together. Though they weren't sufficient in the end, I am forever grateful for the influence his efforts had on me. When I let go of my old beliefs and fears about being a woman, I discovered I actually really *liked* dressing up.

Our last year together was the toughest. We almost ended our relationship just after our fourth anniversary, but last-ditch, dramatic attempts to save it kept us going another year. Our schedules had always been conflicting. Sam worked a daytime office job, and I had been working primarily late-afternoon and evening hours at the Aladdin Theater and as an administrator at an adult Spanish-language school. In addition, I was still working as a professional petsitter, which often required me to stay overnight elsewhere. What if we got on the same schedule? Would we have more time and energy to engage in foreplay and intimacy? My role with the language school was coming to a natural close anyway, and I agreed to take a hiatus from my theater and petsitting work.

I began working daytime hours in an administrative capacity with Living Yoga, a nonprofit that teaches yoga to people in prison and drug and alcohol treatment centers. I loved my new job; I deeply stood behind the mission, and the consistency of the position allowed me to feel financially stable for the first time in years. I definitely had more time and energy for the relationship, but we filled that time with activities other than sex. We'd go out with friends, go dancing or to live music, watch movies in bed. We still avoided sex.

Having enjoyed my women's group so much, and knowing my romantic (or not so romantic) relationship was coming to an end, I strengthened bonds with several women friends. For my thirtieth birthday, I arranged a retreat at the Oregon coast for four friends, who, I learned through our weekend of talking, cooking, drinking wine, and talking some more, were together an eclectic mix: one was a happily married woman who was satisfied with her sex life; one was a happily single woman who *loved* sex—of all kinds, with all genders; and one was a single woman who only loved sex for one. And then there was me, who felt married, about to get divorced, and daily celebrated and struggled with sex. So what did we talk about? Sex, of course. It was by now an easy topic for me to discuss. I recall telling the group that I would really prefer a relationship where neither partner wanted sex. I could do without it. My current relationship made so much sense in all other ways; sex screwed up an otherwise beautiful partnership. Would this be my lot in life?

Though we were in different places and had different attitudes about sex, it was still empowering to share aspects of our intimate lives with each other. Simply opening up a dialogue on what is often a taboo topic creates major shifts in perspective. Again, we found we had a lot more in common than it would at first seem. And when we shared differences, they were respectfully accepted and appreciated. Now, I won't pretend that all women are capable of responding to such honesty and vulnerability in a way that feels safe for all parties. But I will say that our culture has to start somewhere. If we stay quiet and closed out of fear of what others might think or say, our society will stay rooted in sexual repression. And sadly, a sexually repressed society leads to all manner of sexual addiction, violence, and depression. We owe it to ourselves and our community to break this cycle, and we can do it simply by doing one thing—start talking.

We weren't all talk during the weekend retreat, however. The house we rented was right on the beach, and since it was a cold and rainy November, standard Oregon autumn fare, we pretty much had the beach to ourselves. After so much talk about sexuality and celebrating our womanhood—not to mention my thirtieth birthday—we took it as a sign that we should perform some kind of ritual. Obviously, my wine-soaked friends declared, that should be to swim naked in the icy waters of the Pacific Ocean, in broad daylight.

We counted down from five, rapidly stripped naked, and ran screaming into the icy water. I had never experienced such a sense of freedom and release. The sheer frigidity of the water gave me permission to allow my voice to be heard. I screamed like hell, partially because it was so damn cold, but also because it felt so damn good. I had stifled my inner wild woman for so long that it was magical to stand out there, in the ocean, in my most wild, natural state. I was free as the whales, and I felt just as large, for I was not just my body—I was spirit.

15
Letting Go with Grace

ALMOST EXACTLY A year later, I was finally able to admit that my relationship needed to end. The turning point came when I began my first reread of Conversations with God. The books had been lying quietly on the bookshelf, dormant in my mind but present in my soul, over the past five years. Actually, to be honest, they were lying on our toilet shelf—having been placed there by yours truly as a subtle message to Sam that he'd once said he'd read it (I knew where he did his best reading). Turns out it was me that needed the subtle reminder.

Sam was visiting his family in New York for two weeks over the Thanksgiving holiday, providing me an opportunity to distance myself from his energy and reacquaint myself with my own. I found that I was somewhat relieved to be alone. I had all of this extra time and energy to appease my introverted nature. I read all three books in the series during his absence. In some ways, it was as if I were discovering the books for the first time. I had five more years of life experience—and my first real partnership—to use as a backdrop on which to apply these concepts.

The first eye-opener was the concept that relationships with others are about yourself: what can you give, what parts of yourself will you highlight. I realized instantly that all that energy I'd been investing in the relationship had been an effort to hold on to Sam out of fear of losing him. By doing so, I was simultaneously giving up parts of myself in order to complete his picture of who he wanted his partner to be and holding him to my own standards of who I not only wanted my partner to be but thought he should be.

Walsh's theory suggests that we worry about the self only—an idea that runs contradictory to what most of us have been taught—so that the soul may experience the highest form of self. We spend so much time thinking about what the other is doing, thinking, wanting, expecting...when none of that should matter. It only matters what we are being. The highest form of you becomes the highest form of me; the highest form of me becomes the highest form of that person over there—because we are all one.

I remember the moment I allowed that belief to reenter my being. It felt like a tidal wave of energy coursing through my veins, resulting in a euphoric release of pressure and a great state of peace. Yes, it was not unlike an orgasm. I realized I had given up significant parts of myself in the relationship. I had stopped writing, I had curtailed my silliness because it was a turnoff to Sam, I had halted my spiritual practice because I was too busy with him. These were all choices that I had made—and I know that he made similar choices himself—in an effort to please the other. We had sacrificed a lot, and I was exhausted from it. Our story is proof that when we cling to something out of fear, we can't hold on to it.

So, I believe we have to first decide who we really are. If we want to be love in a relationship, how would love react to whatever it is our partner presents us with? What would love do now? That is a powerful question. If I weren't so averse to needles, I would have it tattooed on my wrist...and maybe even my forehead, so that everyone interacting with me would be forced to consider the same question.

Rereading these books allowed me to conceptualize what I had glazed over in the past. What I had feared would be the trap my brother would fall into by entering into marriage was a trap I had fallen into myself. I had allowed limits to be placed on my soul, and I had imposed them on my partner. I had also failed to register that marriage—or partnership—is whatever the agreement is between the people involved. Partnership could instead, when practiced in communion, be used as a tool for each person's soul to reach its highest potential. The partners could recognize that their growth together may be intended to last a lifetime or perhaps only a few months. Reflecting on my own relationship, I now understood that it was appropriate for us to remain together only as long as we grew together. Sam and I had exhausted all attempts to stay together, and our growth had hit a wall.

So, what would love do now? I realized that love would let Sam go—let us go. It was not fair to either of us to ask us to be something we weren't. I wished for him complete joy and happiness, and I knew he could not find that within the partnership that we had created. Likewise, I ached to explore aspects of my own personality that I felt had been stifled by the relationship. I wanted to travel abroad independently again. I wanted to reclaim my playful spirit. I wanted to have sex without all the historical baggage. I wanted to not feel guilty when I chose a night in with a good book over a night out with friends. The possibilities were endless.

Coincidentally—well, not coincidentally, as there are no coincidences—it was on Thanksgiving Day that I reconnected with Boris. Single again, he had moved to London, fulfilling a dream of his he'd shared when we were together six years before. I realized that the mere fact that he'd followed his dream made him even more attractive and intriguing to me. I wanted to get to know this new version of the man I'd known.

Boris had sent me birthday wishes via e-mail a few weeks earlier, and I replied by suggesting we have a video conversation, rather than try to catch up on all the significant changes in our lives over e-mail. We scheduled our chat for the holiday, which provided a welcome respite from my reclusive state.

At first, I was uncomfortably shy. Where do we begin? We'd e-mailed a few times over the years, but it had been several years since we'd used voice or image to communicate. I quietly shared, "This is so strange, it's been so long, there's so much to say, and yet I don't know where to start."

He smiled, and my heart instantly melted. "It will get easier." He spoke with such calm and presence—he already seemed like a wiser and more mature version of the man I remembered. And that accent. Oh, that accent. I wanted to jump through the screen and rub my face in it.

I didn't allow myself to completely indulge in the reprisal of my former fantasy world (girl reunites with former Brazilian lover after years apart; will their love be rekindled?)—I knew there would be a lot of steps toward closure of my current relationship before I could consider if such a possibility with Boris felt right to me. But I did recognize instantly that a different world was available to me—one with intrigue, playfulness, and yes, desire. I could not deny that even through the computer screen, I was physically and emotionally attracted to Boris's body and spirit. I began to remember what it felt like to be with him: the ease, the magnetic pulse. I had held back a lot during that time. What if I saw him now? Would I feel an even deeper attraction and perhaps even *sexual* desire? The seed had been planted, I believe for both of us.

We logged off our call and shortly after sent each other similar messages: "Seeing you again made me realize how much I've missed you." We began to list and compare memories we each had from our time together. Nostalgia was in full bloom. Sam returned home, and I delayed breaking up with him, instead taking comfort in my emails with Boris. It was the easier—and more exciting—route. We shared stories about our current lives and discussed our dreams. We spoke via video call on Christmas, but I was somewhat surprised, on New Year's Day, when he disclosed over online chat that he had some major goals for the new year:

"I've decided I'm coming to visit you in Portland."

What?

I felt a twinge of panic as I thought, *Wait! My boyfriend and I need to break up first!* Part of me was still clinging to the past, waiting for the most appropriate time and manner to have the discussion with Sam. But that time would never come. I grieved deeply, and privately from Sam, for the next two weeks. Thank God I had a supportive coworker with whom I felt comfortable sharing my emotions; the smallest memory or song on the radio would set me off, and the tear floodgates would open with vengeance. I knew Sam would agree with my decision once we had the discussion, but it was still so hard to initiate. But eventually, I revealed what was behind the curtain. I spoke my truth. He had his own similar truth.

We grieved together for a few months. It was an unusual breakup in that we continued living together for three more months. We both needed a gradual transition; our lives had become so entwined. Five years was a significant portion of our lives—how could we just up and divide it? We even went out on a date for Valentine's Day. It was an extremely bittersweet holiday. When I arrived at work in the morning, there was a bouquet of flowers on my desk. I recognized the florist—the unique, whimsical design instantly revealed who they were from, as if I'd had any doubt. Sam had sent me flowers from the same florist on our first Valentine's Day together. I had already begun to cry, but when I read the card, my tears fell full force:

Happy Valentine's Day, to my best friend of the last five years.

It still chokes me up.

Over time we told more and more of our shared friends, our families—and finally ourselves, on a deeper level. It was truly over. Sam left for another week in New

York, and I began moving my stuff out. He would return to a half-empty home.

I left him one final love letter. It was really a letter of gratitude. Gratitude for the role he played in giving me back to myself. He had challenged me to confront my fears, to move beyond shame. Without his encouragement as a catalyst, I don't know that I ever would have engrossed myself so deeply in exploring my old beliefs about sexuality. I would not have become the woman I am today.

Everyone who crosses our path—especially our intimate partners—leaves such a profound impact on our lives. Human relationships represent an interesting paradox in that we are whole and complete unto ourselves in no need of a particular other, but without another to provide a context in which to know ourselves, we are nothing. I am so grateful for those who have crossed my path and allowed me to discover who I am.

16
Choosing My Experience

WITH THE CONCLUSION of my relationship with Sam, I began to seriously play with the idea of visiting Boris in London. His work schedule would not allow him to visit Portland until much later in the year, and besides, I was anxious for a change of scenery. I booked a flight for early spring, to coincide with the London Lindy Exchange—a four-day international swing dance event.

With each conversation in our increased e-mailing and video chatting, my excitement for seeing Boris again was brought to new heights. Our exchanges were not of the overtly romantic sort, as they had been six years before, but rather were laced with a mature understanding that we didn't know what would happen when we were together again. I don't believe either of us was attached to a particular expectation—we simply knew we couldn't wait to see how our energy would mesh after all these years. Seeing each other through videocam, however, provided a good indication that there would be a strong physical attraction, and there was an unspoken but mutual desire for our reunion to be romantic.

We booked a weekend trip to Paris—only two hours away by train. He had never been to Paris, and I was aching to return after having briefly visited the city while studying abroad in college. When he e-mailed me the train ticket confirmation, and I saw our names listed next to each other, a pleasurable warmth flowed throughout my body. I couldn't believe this was happening. I was visiting my parents in La Crosse when I received the e-mail; I was sitting at the same computer desk I'd been at when I anxiously chatted with Boris upon returning from Buenos Aires six years before. Life was so funny.

During that same visit, I disclosed to my parents that I was planning another international trip. Each time I would share my latest travel plans with my parents, they would grow quiet and anticipate with fear which country they considered a Third World one in crisis I would be visiting this time. When I responded with London, England, I felt their discernible sigh of relief.

"Oh! What are you going to do in London?"

"A Brazilian," I wanted to reply but of course did not.

"I'm going there for the London Lindy Exchange," I instead divulged. Then casually added, "Do you remember my friend Boris, from Brazil? He lives in London now, so I have a free place to stay."

That's why I will be seeing Boris, after all, I thought jokingly. *A free place to stay.* I chuckled to myself at my little secret.

"Oh yes, I remember talking to him on the phone," my mom grew excited. "He sounded sexy. Is he?"

My mom had grown more comfortable over the years with the idea of her daughter engaging in sexual activity—I was now over thirty years old, after all—but I don't think either of my parents considered that our relationship was of the sexual sort. It had taken a year for them to start calling Sam my boyfriend. They'd ask me how my friend was doing—even well after they knew that Sam and I were living together. Surely they assumed we were sharing the same bed. It was still hard, I believe, for my parents to view their daughter in an adult light. Children likely always remain children in their parents' eyes—an understanding that escaped me during most of my formative years but that no longer triggers me. It's a natural part of parenthood, I suppose.

When my brother and his wife arrived at my parents' house the following day, I dodged more travel questions. I had not researched any particular tourist destinations and found it hard not to divulge that I was actually going to visit a former lover. The lindy exchange became my default answer when asked by anyone but my closest friends.

Though I may not have been completely open with my parents about the romantic nature of my trip, I did open up on my spirituality. When my dad asked me what political party I now supported, I could feel his energy prepare for confrontation, remembering the way I used to respond to political debates. But this time, I spoke a different truth. I was able to remain calm and confidently state that, actually, I did not affiliate myself with *any* party or candidate. I watched the firm press of his lips soften and his eyebrows relax into a neutral state.

"So, you mean, you're an Independent?" He appeared grateful that I was at least not self-identifying as a supporter of the current Democrat leader, allowing him to set aside a few bullets he'd been ready to expel.

"Well, no, not that either."

"Wait, I don't understand." His eyebrows now sank in a brow furrowed with confusion.

not argue with. Call it our individual intuition call it our personal truth. We simply *can't* argue with that. The case was closed. My dad accepted that although he had not gotten me to support his political party, at least I was not standing behind his opponent. He rose from the table in silence, the last remnants of steam dissipating from the crevices of his ears. Later that night, he calmly approached me, gave me a hug, and said, "I love you, Becs." I had never doubted it.

That night marked a significant turning point in the way I communicate with my family. Always, *always,* when we come from love and speak our truth, progress is made. I'd come a long way since those days after returning from Argentina six years before. So had my dad.

SOON AFTER I returned to Portland from my family visit, the Universe sent me an opportunity to attend a five-day spiritual retreat with Neale Donald Walsch in southern Oregon. Shortly after rereading his book series and experiencing personal epiphanies as a result, I signed up for the author's e-newsletter list. The first message I received announced that his annual *free* retreat was about to be held. All I needed to do was register and arrange my own housing and transportation. By then I was better accustomed to paying attention to signs from the Universe, and this one was obvious. I needed to go to this retreat. I had been quoting Neale Donald Walsch so regularly when offering support to and philosophizing with friends that instead of asking for *my* advice, they'd ask me, "What would Neale say?"

After telling my family about the retreat, they asked with concern, "He's not going to brainwash you, is he?"

My response was an eager, "I hope so!" I could not think of any better belief system to be brainwashed by. After years of societal impact, don't all of our brains need a good cleansing?

And thus, with a hopeful attitude and an open mind, I arrived at the retreat where I began my deeper emergence into the rich spiritual world that had been available to me all along—had I only allowed the opportunity for it to shine through. For those five days—some of which ran for twelve hours—I sat in an intimate room with about sixty other beautiful souls and listened to Neale respond to question after question with grace, compassion, and humor, not to mention divine wisdom. Though I had extreme appreciation for the knowledge this man bestowed upon the world through his writings, I had never placed him on a pedestal or thought of him as a guru. After meeting him, it was clear that he never would have placed himself in that category either. He was innately human, the first to admit his faults and his wayward path toward arriving at where he was today—which he still believed to be far from master status. He was simply a messenger, albeit a very good one.

I soaked up his presence with great thirst. I hung on his every word, integrating each response into my being so that I could be a messenger of these lessons that have so impacted my life as well. Ever the ready student, I found myself fighting the urge to say, "I'll take this one,

Neale," when hearing someone pose a question that had either already been answered or that I remembered well from his books. I could not get enough. I found that this deep exploration of the emotional and spiritual world seemed to give me an unlimited supply of energy.

Perception was a big concept of the retreat and under its umbrella is the momentous idea that there are no victims or villains. Even Holocaust sufferers had the choice to view themselves as victims—or not. They could even choose to see themselves as chosen ones, as people whose spirits were so strong that God selected them to experience such extreme cruelty because God knew they could handle it. They were strong enough to sacrifice their lives—or to survive to tell their tales—as a magnificent message to the world.

And if there are no victims, then there can be no villains. Hitler was a messenger sent to earth to teach us about ourselves. Under just one man's influence, people were persuaded to commit genocide—of a group that Jesus belonged to. What does that say about humanity? Hitler showed us who we are capable of becoming, if we give more weight to a source of truth outside of ourselves rather than what we know to be true in our hearts. The Holocaust was made possible by the cooperative submission of millions of people—people who had lost consciousness of who they were. It is sad, but true, that it took such massive killing to show humanity to itself—whereas Jesus showed us our highest potential, Hitler showed us our lowest.

And if Hitler wasn't a villain, I certainly wasn't either. Finally, I could fully release the shame I had held inside me regarding the court trial in Nashville. The trial, and my role in it, had played out perfectly in accordance with what each of our souls was seeking to experience. How could I be so bold as to claim that my lack of certainty in the courtroom was more critical than the conspiring of the entire Universe itself? Rather, my role was *part* of the Universe's plan—I needed to experience myself as who I am not, in order to know who I truly am. Finding my voice has gotten much easier since then. I can only surmise what purpose the whole situation had for the two brothers involved, but I can accept with conviction that it was perfectly what it was meant to be.

Despite the turmoil I allowed the experience of the trial to wreak on my body and spirit, I am grateful I had it. Had I not moved out of the house I'd been living in and into the house with my dancing roommates, I may never have begun to explore blues dancing—and that is something I cannot imagine my life without. There are numerous other circumstances of my life that that incident influenced as well. I may have even been drawn to my job with Living Yoga as a result of that incident. The organization offers tools for personal change to people in prison and recovery and also hope and compassion for those people our society would often rather forget about. My work may not have directly affected the men that were involved in my criminal case, but I like to believe that by helping to offer these services to one community, a more expansive love and compassion for people who have made mistakes disseminates all over the world. We are, after all, all one.

My favorite metaphor for this concept is the following: imagine looking through a microscope and seeing the breakdown of matter into tiny particles. The stronger the microscope, the more division of particles you can see. In fact, you can never *stop* breaking down these particles—there is an infinite number of smaller and smaller parts. Now, imagine the reverse effect. Put the sum of the parts all together, and you have, for example, an organ inside your body, your whole body, your body inside a house, a house inside a village, a village inside a country, a planet, the universe.

With that said, when we hurt another, we are hurting parts of ourselves. When we destroy nature, we are destroying parts of ourselves. When we hurt ourselves, we are hurting other people, destroying a piece of nature. So what does it take to break this cycle of competition—for resources, for love, for power? To truly believe that we are one and that there is enough—of whatever it is we are seeking. Everything everyone needs is already available—we need only share it.

These are very large concepts that can seem overwhelming if we view them through the lens of needing a global shift in order to experience real change here on our planet. The good news is that, as Ghandi so eloquently stated, all we have to do is "be the change we wish to see in the world." Thom Hartmann, in his book *The Last Hours of Ancient Sunlight,* stated that only 7 percent of the people on this planet joining together with the same intention and purpose is enough to start a revolution. Recent movements and the popularity of new spiritual thought waves assure me that we're getting closer to that revolution.

With all of these new powerful paradigm shifts, the retreat wrapped up, and I returned to Portland inspired to share my experience with others. I had a goal of building my public speaking confidence, so that I could someday share these spiritual messages on a grander scale. A friend recommended that I try Toastmasters, a nonprofit club with the purpose of developing public speaking skills through practice and feedback. I chose a club that met in a location convenient to me that consisted of young professionals. I had been told I need not participate in the group my first night, that I may merely observe.

Regardless, I was quite nervous. I chatted online with Boris right beforehand. He offered, "I'll be right there in the room with you, holding your hand." If only he had known how close that would be to the truth.

Each meeting upholds a strict agenda. A portion is scheduled for impromptu speeches, where one member selects another member to speak for around three minutes on a topic just announced. I figured there was no way I would be selected; it was my first night, so they wouldn't do that to me, right? The St. Patrick's Day holiday had recently passed, and the night revolved around this theme.

"Tell us about your most memorable St. Patrick's Day," the man responsible for selecting his prey began. "Rebecca."

WTF?

I am not one for being able to process and think on my feet. I'm an introvert—I prefer carefully outlining my stories and opinions with pen and paper, quietly alone with my thoughts. Then maybe, just *maybe,* if I'm really proud and certain of what I wrote, I'll share it with close friends. When I get unexpectedly called on in a meeting or other group environment, I am able to find words…but they're not my most eloquent and thoughtful words. Often, I regret these words even before they come out of my mouth—*Don't say that!* my mind shouts, knowing full well that I will—because the only thing more embarrassing than saying the words that are accessible to me is not saying anything at all. Silence is a definite sign of inferiority and nervousness—or so I believed in that moment.

I needed *something* to say, and I needed it fast. Having only one memory of the holiday, as it is not one that I usually celebrate, I told my story about meeting a Brazilian man in a hostel in Buenos Aires, ditching the hostel for a private hotel room, and making love after sharing a bottle of wine. I spared the room the intimate details, but nonetheless I recall thinking as I told my story, *I can never see these people again!* I mean, really…I just made myself sound like an easy catch to a room full of people I'd just met.

Thus far, the Toastmaster speakers that night had all presented in a very controlled, intellectual manner. They used fancy words and carefully orchestrated gestures. They began their speeches by welcoming their "fellow Toastmasters and esteemed guest" (me). Then I stepped up there and enthusiastically rendered the equivalent of

"If you really want to know what I believe in now, Dad, a better question to ask is what my spiritual beliefs are. I believe the main problem on our planet is not an economic or political problem but a spiritual problem." I watched him try to anticipate where this would lead.

I continued, "Everything boils down to how we view ourselves in relation to others, and in relation to God, or whatever we choose to call the Divine spirit. We can attempt to "fix" individual problems on a nonspiritual level, but in reality we're just placing Band-Aids over wounds. I, therefore, choose not to put my faith in one human being—one political leader—to "save" us. Instead, I believe any change toward a more peaceful world has to start within each of us. I cast a "vote" each time I interact with someone, with the way I treat people and the choices I make regarding my own reactions to the way others treat me. I try to disseminate as much joy and love as I can, every moment of every day. Therefore, what I believe spiritually has a domino effect on every choice I make, including decisions that our culture likes to categorize as economic or political. I'm not saying your way or your beliefs are wrong, Dad—it's just different from what I believe and how I choose to live my life."

"So, let me ask you this. What is your news source?" He was sure that I had simply been indoctrinated by unworthy and unreliable media. His face began to tighten again, in preparation for battle.

"My intuition, Dad," I replied.

He swallowed the words he'd been planning to discharge, and his jaw relaxed. I'd stated a claim he could a drunken campfire story. Could I still be an esteemed guest after that?

Had I told the same story to a group of my friends, I am sure it would have been met with interest and appreciation. This group, however, wasn't playing any games. They politely clapped at the end, which was customary Toastmasters procedure, but not one person cracked a smile. As was also customary, my speech later received feedback from the emcee of the night; I nervously awaited my doom but was met with a surprising response.

"Rebecca, first of all, congratulations on getting up here on your first night—you are already braver than many people who have come to these clubs. Second, you presented yourself in a very authentic way; we already have a good picture of who you are—well done!" She continued to offer feedback on how to better use my hands and to notice my filler words, such as *umm*, but overall it was very inspiring feedback. I did wonder, *Wait, what picture of who I am did she perceive?* but I let it go. It didn't matter. My fear around seeing these people again was simply just that—fear. My old pattern of thinking.

I realized I didn't have to fit within the framework of how everybody else gave a speech. I just needed to be me. I had a spirit and a story worth sharing. I couldn't control others' reactions, but I could control my own—and I chose to be proud that I'd allowed myself to be vulnerable. Well done, indeed!

17
If Only My Sex Therapist Could See Me Now

IN THE WEEKS leading up to my trip to London, I started to feel a slight disconnect between Boris and me. Our communication was less frequent and our topics less intimate. I started to consider that he may have met someone. My ego responded to the hypothetical scenario with disappointment and jealousy, but I was so much better equipped to notice and respond to those emotions now. I realized I could choose my experience. What if he really *had* met someone? What would that mean for me? I decided to make peace with the idea. I could choose to be happy for him. Would I still go to London? Well, I guess I didn't need to consider that question until I knew if my suspicion was even true.

Meanwhile, I continued about my life as usual. Which meant that on Tuesday nights, I was out blues dancing. One time I was floating about the room, absorbed in my element, when an attractive Eastern European man I had not seen before asked me to dance. "Sure!" I gave my regular enthusiastic reply.

He introduced himself.

"Hi, I'm Boris."

You're who? I laughed to myself. This was strange.

"Oh. I have a friend named Boris, who I met in Argentina." I couldn't resist disclosing at least a little bit.

"You've been to Argentina?! Have you been to Iguazú Falls?"

This just got weirder.

"Yes..." I answered tentatively. Was this someone's idea of a cryptic joke?

"I was there about six years ago. It's so beautiful there!"

"Hmmm. I was there six years ago as well."

And so the conversation continued...for four more dances.

"What else are you into, besides dancing?" he asked.

"Well, I practice yoga, I bike—"

"You do yoga? I'm taking a yoga teacher training with the founder of Living Yoga," he interrupted with surprise.

"That's interesting. I work for Living Yoga."

He stared at me in awe, and must have taken all these synchronicities as a sign. "I don't want to be too presumptuous, but can I take you out to lunch?"

For the last five years, I had an automatic response to this question on the rare occasion that it had happened: "Sorry, I have a boyfriend." Now, my heart began to race. I was so used to dodging this question—either because I wasn't single, or because I simply wasn't interested. But now, I really had no legitimate reason to say no.

"Uhhhhh, I don't *know*...I just got out of a five-year relationship..." I stopped myself from adding, "And there's this other Boris I'm meeting up with in London in a few weeks..."

"Well then, perfect timing," he replied. I admired his boldness. "Come on, it's just lunch."

That's true. It was just lunch. This guy was good.

I agreed to lunch the following week, and we bid farewell, but not until he called after me, "Congratulations on the breakup!"

Again, a bold response. I liked it. I was tired of being met with sympathetic eyes and an "I'm sorry" after telling people who didn't know me well that my relationship had ended. *I* wasn't sorry. I had given myself space to grieve, and both Sam and I had made a conscious choice to set each other free to experience greater happiness. I was excited for this new phase.

The timing of this new man in my life was impeccable. I had just moved out of Sam's place, and the day after Boris 2 (as he would affectionately come to be known among my close friends) asked me out, I received a very carefully and respectfully written e-mail from Boris. He had met someone.

Though the boundaries of their relationship weren't yet determined, he was experiencing a deep sense of conflict and at the very least did not think it appropriate to go on a romantic trip to Paris with me anymore. I lost my breath for a moment, but I quickly regained it. I closed my eyes and then began to laugh. Of *course* he would meet someone now, just a few weeks before my arrival. And of course the Universe would plant this seed of a different man in my life now as well, who just happened to have the name Boris. What a joke! What was the Universe trying to tell me? I concluded that whatever its message, it had a great sense of humor.

I wrote Boris back an equally compassionate and respectful e-mail. I still wanted to visit him. I had the lindy exchange to attend, and in any regard, I shared that we had remained in touch over all this time and distance for certainly more reasons than sex. I admired so many other qualities in him that I desired in my friends as well, and we could shift our perspective to be one of simply a friendly visit. He agreed he still wanted me to come and that I could still stay in the extra bedroom, so we moved forward with our plans—excluding Paris.

Meanwhile, I prepared for my first date with Boris 2. While arranging plans for lunch by phone, we realized dinner actually worked better with our schedules. So, it was no longer, "just lunch," but I was okay with that. I was quite nervous—it was my first date in over five years! How does one do this again? My good friend Julie was an amazing source of support, as always. She was my soul sister—the one with whom I could share all the details of my life, including my strong spiritual beliefs that others weren't always comfortable discussing. We were both signed up for Neale Donald Walsch's daily inspirational e-mails, which always begin, "On this day of your life, I believe God wants you to know…" Channeling Walsch's spirit, Julie sent me this glorious text message just as I was arriving for my date:

> *On this day of your life, Rebecca, I believe God wants you to know that you're going to have a HOT night! And even if you don't, remember that you and this night are perfect. Embrace it for what it is, which is everything and nothing.*

Thank you, Julie. Just what I needed. As it turned out,

that first night didn't get all that hot. We had dinner, at which we learned we felt more comfortable with party chitchat than longer conversation with each other, followed by dessert and a quick, uninspiring kiss goodnight. Still, we made plans for a second date the following weekend.

Now *that* night, things did get hot.

We met up at a movie theater downtown to see a new Chilean film. We sat in the back row, perhaps both of us indicating we felt the first date was not a good representation of what we wanted from the other. We weren't alone in the back row, but that didn't stop us. About twenty minutes into the movie, the sexual chemistry sparked. He mistook my tug on his jacket (I was cold) for a sign that I wanted to pull him in for a kiss. I didn't mind being mistaken. Damn, that was a good kiss. Add Polish kiss to my repertoire of famed international foreplay.

We were like two horny teenagers. He gently moved my hair and began kissing my neck in such a way I had not experienced in oh so very long—if ever, as I was now more open to responding to physical intimacy. I melted into his touch. I allowed his hand to slowly browse along the back of my neck to the front and tenderly down my dress, where it rested upon my breast.

I didn't care that we were likely being watched—in fact, I am sure that added to the thrill. My eyes closed, my head leaned back, my breath grew deeper and my heart rate faster. Oh, thank you, God. It had been so long since I'd been touched in a way that truly turned me on. There was no emotional baggage between us, and—I realized—

no emotional baggage *within* me. I felt no shame, no fear, no feelings of inadequacy. I simply felt physical *bliss*. I couldn't wait for the movie to end.

But now, where to go? I didn't have my own place yet, and he had just moved into a house in the suburbs with no furniture. We were a couple of wandering souls. We decided to go for a drive. It was approaching 10:00 p.m. We arrived at the entrance to Washington Park—a beautiful park with a gorgeous view of the city—just as a police officer was about to close the gate. He motioned for us to roll our window down, and he leaned in.

"Where are you folks going?"

Boris 2 took the reins. "Well, we were going to go to the park."

"Well, sorry, folks, the park closes at ten."

"Oh," Boris 2 reluctantly replied. "Well, do you know any good make-out spots?"

I laughed. I looked at him in disbelief but also with great pride. I loved his audacity. Thankfully, the officer did too.

"Well, Washington Park *is* a good one, but unfortunately you can't go there now. But just continue driving up Burnside Street and pull over. You'll be fine up there." I noticed the ring on the officer's finger. I suspected he was nostalgic for his earlier days. He wished us well.

And so up the hill we went, and there, in the back of his hatchback, we consummated our evening. It was great fun, especially when he stepped out of the car to get something from the driver's seat, with no shirt and unzipped pants—just as another car went by, shining its lights on the spectacle (or should I say, testicle?) For once, I was "that" girl—the naughty one in the backseat of the car. It felt tantalizingly sweet.

And so our relationship continued for the next couple of weeks. We would meet up for dinner, followed by "dessert" back at his place. We got creative with the lack of furniture; or shall I say, we made good use of counter space. The bathroom counter was my favorite, as we could watch ourselves in the mirror. I'd never done that before. I loved it. I didn't recognize myself, and yet I did. That beautiful, sexy woman was *me*. My affirmations had come a long way in internalizing these new beliefs about myself. I was so grateful that I could recognize the beauty—and the perfection—in imperfection.

Nearing the conclusion of one night's adventures, we noticed blood on the condom. I had not been expecting my period so soon. I didn't think much of it, but Boris 2 looked a bit shocked.

"Wait. Are you *menstruating*?"

I chuckled at his choice of vocabulary and casually replied, "Well, it appears that I am."

He was quiet.

"Do you have a problem with that?" I followed up with curiosity.

"Well, I'm not going to stop *now*," he replied with disdain. "But I don't normally have sex during menstruation."

My old self would have been hurt and likely would have deeply internalized the sensation of shame. But not *this* woman.

"Wow. You don't know what you're missing! I'm most horny when I'm on my period," I replied, without the slightest embarrassment.

"When are you *not* horny?" was his reply.

I laughed with great joy. Music to my ears. If only my sex therapist could see me now!

I had been upfront from the start that I was not looking for a committed relationship. He'd sighed in relief, as he wasn't either. Not to mention, I did not feel connected to him beyond a physical level. But the physical was all I needed at that point in my life. I needed to have fun with sex; I needed to not take it so seriously. I was again reminded of a line from *Before Sunset,* in which Jesse described how, in our thirties, sex no longer has to be viewed as a life-altering event.

I'd had my first real "rebound" relationship. I was now ready for bigger and deeper aspects of love and partnership.

III
Finding Ecstasy

18
Boris's World

THE DAY OF my flight to London finally arrived. My fantasy world of what it would be like to reunite with Boris had been tamed by the shift in perspective to visiting as friends, but I was nonetheless incredibly excited to see him. I was happy for him that he'd met someone with whom he felt an intimate connection. *Who am I to deny him the experience of love?* I thought. Regardless of my understanding that he did not intend to pursue me romantically during my visit, I remained open to the possibility that more could transpire. My belief system now encompassed the view that we need to be true to ourselves first. Boris needed to decide for himself what was "right" or "wrong" for him, and I trusted myself to respond with the action in line with my own truth. And so it was with an open heart and mind that I arrived, after an overnight flight, at his door.

DAY 1

It was a sunny Friday afternoon, rather warm for early spring. It was a day I'd normally ache to spend outside, perhaps soaking in the sun's rays while watching the ducks rummage for scraps in the canal across from Boris's building, which I was fast approaching in an airport taxi. But today, all I could think about was reaching a bed. I needed a long nap before my plans for the night would commence, and before I could be fully present to engage in conversation with Boris once he arrived home from work.

My eyes scanned the address numbers until they landed upon a long, red-brick building that the taxi driver confirmed was the address I'd given him. Thanking the driver and collecting my luggage, I stepped up inside the picturesque alcove that marked the entryway to Boris's unit. The key was left for me outside the door, as Boris and his housemates were still at work. I'd been unable to contact Boris to let him know I'd arrived safely, but I knew he'd find me soon enough. I turned the key to the heavy wooden door, relieved when it gracefully cracked open. I was actually somewhat surprised—as if I would get this close and still not be allowed to enter Boris's world. But here I was. I recognized the room from photos of parties and dinners held there. I glanced around at all the open wine and beer bottles. *Definitely a bachelor pad.* I smiled.

I set my luggage down at the base of the steps, a large, heavy backpack that was the same one I'd traveled with to Argentina. I had since meticulously sewed patches of flags along the sides, representing each country the backpack had been to. I wanted my backpack to represent me, or at least the vision of myself that I hoped observers would construe of me upon noticing the bag. World traveler, likely a speaker of multiple languages, free spirit. Not necessarily American: the Argentinean flag was displayed most prominently. I coveted being imagined more exotic than I felt.

Free of the weight of my bags, I slowly climbed up the first flight of stairs with my head raised inquisitively high. Though I knew I was alone, I felt a sensation of being watched. The first open door had to be the spare bedroom, where I would sleep. I was anxious to get the bed ready to climb into and finally be able to rest, but I wanted to explore alone a bit before that...I wanted to find his room.

I went up another flight of stairs and found what I suspected was Boris's room because of what I saw inside. It was the only one with the door ajar, as if, I decided, Boris was saying that I may observe without feeling like an intruder. I noticed a skull handkerchief across the desk. The smell was that of late-night bars: the slight aroma of cigarette smoke, though I knew he wasn't a smoker himself, and the mixture of cologne and sweat. It was not unpleasant, merely a strong indication of masculine energy. An open vodka bottle sat on the floor by the bed. *Wow*—I chuckled—*must have been a rough night*. I withdrew the single step I'd cautiously taken into the room and went back downstairs to bring my luggage to my room.

After four hours of intermittent sleep and gazing out the window at the abundance of planes in various paths of flight, still not quite believing that one had just brought me here, I heard the front door open and footsteps quickly dash up the stairs. The previous moments of solitude and quiet contemplation were welcomingly transformed into bountiful and joyous energy with Boris's eager exclamation of, "*Ohhhhhhhh!*" as he darted into the room and planted multiple, rapid kisses on my neck and cheeks, breathing in my presence with unbridled enthusiasm. I had fantasized many times over the past few months what this first encounter would be like. It played out even more perfectly in reality.

I was only half awake. I stretched and laughed at his exuberance as he settled alongside my body in bed. He was still wearing his jacket, a black leather coat I recognized from photos. I was still wearing my flight clothes I'd dressed in what was now the day before: gray yoga pants and a sky-blue tank top. I'd hoped to have time to freshen up before his arrival, but I relinquished my desire to show him the best version of my physical self. This was me, in this moment, I submitted. I snuggled beneath the crook of his arm. My eyes closed to offer myself a moment of internal privacy to take in the moment, but I was acutely aware that he was watching me intently. His hand rested on my stomach and stroked it with desire. After a moment of deliberation, I watched his body make the decision to pursue me. He leaned forward and kissed me in the way I remembered so well. It felt like an intentional test of time; was the magic still there? His head leaned back in pleasure; my soft smile indicated that I felt it too.

I was surprised he was so instantly open to being with me in this capacity. I'd been expecting a demeanor more akin to friendship, after his avowal that he'd recently met someone with whom he was considering a committed relationship. As if he read my mind, he mumbled, "I shouldn't be doing this. Well, I had a couple of drinks with my colleagues."

I loved his touch and his affection, though I was still feeling a bit shy and needed to wrap my cognizance around being there with him after all this time—and to reshift my expectation that we'd be reuniting as friends only. Clearly, there was a history and chemistry more powerful than we'd expected. His advances continued and accelerated, and I gladly accepted them but still needed time…not only to process the moment but to fully awaken from my nap. I excused myself to the bathroom, stepping out from the covers to be met with his excitement as he took in more of my body. He only half-jokingly asked if he could enter the bathroom with me, but in response to my giggle, he settled for standing outside the door. When I emerged, he seized my body, and his tongue found mine once again. His hands around my waist mischievously dared me to just try and walk away.

"Wow, look at you. You're so beautiful."

"You are too. You look the same." I took in his body as well. I'd forgotten how perfectly it melded to mine; his stature and breadth offered a convenient and comfortable embrace.

I sluggishly asked for us to return to the bed, as I was still overcome with jet lag and exhaustion. We lay together a while longer, soaking up each other's presence, before hearing his roommate Alex arrive home. We noted the time and stepped into logistics mode. I had a dance event to attend, and he was going to his roommate Jakub's band gig. Boris followed me to my backpack. He was talking about plans for the night in between kissing me, all the while caressing my waist just below my pant line. It was bliss. His response to me was automatic, subconscious—and my experience was of extreme comfort and pleasure. I recognized the return of passion to my life, to an extent that I hadn't experienced since...well, the last time I'd been with him. His touch was not driven by sex alone; it was enveloped with infatuation, compassion, and tenderness. I still don't know if it's because he's Latino, or because he's simply *him* and I'm *me*.

I asked for a towel, and he realized he would need to buy another, as he only had one—more evidence of a true bachelor.

"Oh! I haven't given you a tour either!" He led me up the next flight of stairs.

"You can use this bathroom to shower. I don't know if you noticed, but there is no shower curtain downstairs. At our last party, someone tore it down." His tone revealed an element of disgust for this particular party guest. He gave me a hand towel, which I assured him would be sufficient until we could buy another.

"And this is my room. Well, it's small, but it's all I need." I welcomed the deeper exploration of where he spent his nights. He drew my attention to the *fileteado* painting we'd picked out together in Buenos Aires, resting atop his dresser. It felt as though he'd been waiting to point it out to me since he'd placed it there when he'd moved in.

He gave me a quick tour of his roommates' rooms before I stepped into the bathroom to freshen up. As I exited from the shower, Boris's door was wide open. He stood shirtless with his foot up on the bed, jamming loudly on his guitar to blues music piped through his phone. I took in his body even further; his dark chest hair accentuated his "wild man" look. Such a rock star. He'd forever be considered in my mind "my crazy Brazilian."

Alex began calling for Boris; he was in a hurry to get to Jakub's show. The two of them helped configure a cell phone for me, which would become my lifesaver for navigating the complex streets of London over the next twelve days, and we parted ways. Boris started down the stairs with Alex, only to run back up and kiss me goodbye, now that he had me alone for a moment. It was a charming gesture of intimacy. I stayed at his home a bit longer to review my route to the dance. I finally stepped out into the city, ready to tackle the tube.

I arrived at the dance, proud that I'd found my way there alone. I quickly made friends with the woman next to me in the queue; I reveled in being the foreigner again. It's so much easier to generate interest from others when you speak with an accent. When I finally made it into the ballroom, I stood back and gazed at the London Lindy Exchange banner hung proudly above the stage. I smiled. I was in London. I was in Boris's city.

I FOUND MY way home shortly after midnight. The tube's hours dictated my travel times, until I learned how to navigate the more complex bus system. Boris arrived shortly after and joined me in my room, where we exchanged news on our respective nights. The sexual energy we had experienced earlier was still building. But I was tired; I asked for a T-shirt of his to sleep in, as I could not locate a sleep shirt of my own amid the pile of strewn clothing I had unpacked earlier. Several minutes went by before he returned,

"Sorry that took me so long. I wanted to find this shirt." He extended a black T-shirt out to me, the word *Quilmes* across the front. I threw my head back in delight. He'd known I would remember this popular brand of beer from Buenos Aires.

I changed out of my dress and into his shirt and my yoga pants. He confessed to not being able to resist me in yoga pants. We shared some passionate kissing before lying on the bed. Things physically progressed in a direction my body wanted but my spirit was not yet ready to receive. I asked that we wait at least until after our first night before making love. I needed some time to reconnect with him emotionally, not just physically.

"I'll be here almost two weeks," I stated, as an attempt to reassure him that we had plenty of time to enjoy each other's bodies. I knew even before I said it, however, that the days would pass quickly, and it was not like me to put off a desire for the elusive "tomorrow." Time didn't really exist, I believed; all we are ever guaranteed is the moment of now. But I said it anyway, to offer a reason for my hesitation. I was not yet ready to divulge in words the part of my soul that yearned to connect with much more than just his body.

"I know," he agreed.

We continued to lie together, however, for some time, stroking each other's bodies, coming to know them again. When he gracefully lifted my shirt and his eyes landed upon my breasts for the first time since Argentina, he seemed in awe, sighing in exclamation, as if he were discovering me for the very first time.

"Do you remember me?" I asked. My heart knew he did, but my mind kept interfering with the reminder that six years had somehow passed.

"Of course," he replied. "I remember how good it was."

I knew he was sincere, yet it was hard for me to accept that the person I was sexually at that time could have offered a man pleasure, especially to such a degree that he'd remember it vividly six years later. I had felt so inept at the time—so inexperienced, like a fraud—not really a woman. Yet he'd never viewed me as anything but. And here I was with him now, no longer that person. I knew I was a sexual woman now. I was not afraid to be vulnerable, knowing I had nothing to be embarrassed or ashamed of and nothing to apologize for. I was simply me, and I was beautiful.

"You know, I still have the note you left under my pillow at the hostel in Iguazú Falls."

"Really? Do you remember what it says?" I had forgotten.

"Of course I do." His tone revealed the assertion that I had asked a ridiculous question. "I've looked at it many times over the years. It said, *I miss you already. Rebby.*"

A sweet cloud of tenderness hung in the air before Boris rose from the bed and leaned over me. With a final kiss, he retreated to his room for the night. I was so glad I had come.

19
Energy at Play

Day 2

I awoke at 11:00 a.m. on Saturday, grateful to have gotten a good night's rest. I heard Boris and Jakub moving around in the kitchen below. It sounded like there was breakfast pending, and I was hungry. From the top of the stairs, I made eye contact with Boris, who was leaning against the wall at the base of the stairs, eating a banana. He stood straight to welcome me and guided me to the kitchen table, where he proudly presented to me in Spanish, "*Medialunas con marmelada de durazno, jugo de naranja, y café con leche.*" I burst out laughing at the gesture—it was the same breakfast we had every day at our hostel in Buenos Aires. He had also made omelets; I couldn't wait to dig in. The three of us sat down for a quiet, leisurely breakfast.

Or so we thought. Only a couple of minutes passed before we jumped at the sound of someone pounding on the kitchen window across from us, screaming, "Ahhh!" with glee, and holding up a case of beer in each hand. Alex was home from the night before. And he brought along four new friends. They burst inside; Alex set down the beer and ran upstairs to bring down his stereo speakers. He turned on the party strobe lights as electronica music filled the room. I looked at Boris; his look was one of uncomfortable restraint. So much for a peaceful breakfast. We ate quicker than planned and retreated to his room—on the third floor, it was the quietest place in the house. Though it was a challenge in the moment to not be annoyed by the unexpected turn of events, we recognized the potential for a good story and accepted our position as merely cogs in the wheel.

We tried to drown out the electronica music with blues while getting ready to explore London a bit. We gratefully bid farewell to Alex's guests and took the bus to Brick Lane. It was my first time riding one of London's famous red double-decker buses. We rushed to the front row of the upper level for the best view. We found more entertainment, however, from listening to a British lady down below loudly detailing her day to another passenger. Boris leaned in toward me, "Even now, a year after moving here, I still feel like I'm watching a Monty Python movie." Despite Boris's observation, I had begun to notice a distinct change in his own pronunciation of English words. His endearing Brazilian accent was already becoming influenced by British overtones. I found him slightly more difficult to understand than before, although his knowledge of the English language had substantially improved. Together we amused ourselves with contemplating the origin of unusual names the driver recited as upcoming bus stops.

"I mean, Nunhead! What is that?" Boris laughed incredulously and I along with him.

Eventually we reached our stop and walked the remainder of the route to Brick Lane, taking in the aromas of various international food stalls, as well as the occasional whiff of patchouli. Before long, we were hungry for lunch and stepped inside a covered market, where we joyously sampled all kinds of global delicacies. We settled on sharing a vegetarian Ethiopian platter on the back patio.

"Have I ever told you my worst first date story?" I inquired mischievously. Ethiopian food always made me recall one particular evening. He welcomed my story and listened without interjection—just appreciated smiles that matched mine, raised eyebrows, and palm slaps to his head.

"I was taken out to dinner by a dancer in Nashville. He knew I was vegetarian, so he made the assumption that any restaurant I'd choose would be completely vegetarian—which was funny, because at the time there were no *strictly* vegetarian restaurants in Nashville. He admitted that he'd eaten a whole steak just before picking me up, so he was sure to get his meat in.

"When we arrived at my chosen Ethiopian restaurant and he saw the menu, he was thrilled that there were meat options. He ordered a chicken platter, and he was so pleased with this new flavor that he ordered another. I was shocked but didn't say anything.

"We had made plans to go swing dancing downtown after dinner. Arriving at the dance club, he immediately excused himself to the bathroom. Ten long minutes later, he exited the bathroom and said, 'I think I need to go home.' His stomach was, naturally, quite unhappy at this point. I welcomed the suggestion to end the night.

"He drove me home, and I sincerely hoped he would just drop me off. Instead, he asked to use my bathroom. And there he remained for, literally, the next half hour.

Upon finally exiting, he advised, 'I wouldn't go in there if I were you.' I laughed nervously, trying to be considerate. I walked him to the door, and he actually expected a *kiss*. I couldn't do it. I opened the door and ushered him out—with a smile and cheerful goodbye, of course."

"Ohhhhh. Poor guy," Boris exclaimed. We laughed together, but felt genuine remorse and compassion for this man's experience.

We continued sharing stories. We had by now known each other for six years; we knew intimate details of each other, but there remained an abundance of beguiling stories to share. We'd so far taken no pictures of us together in London, and I felt a strong desire to capture the moment. I sat beside him for a self-portrait and then stood to sit back across from him. I'd barely stepped away before he somewhat anxiously reached for my arm.

"No, stay."

My heart fluttered. He didn't have to say anything more. I'd been seeking physical closeness with him all day. Despite our intimacy the night before, I still sensed a great deal of conflict in him. I knew he was struggling with not wanting to hurt the woman he had recently met, and I didn't want to confuse him more by reaching out each moment I ached to touch him. I had considered that perhaps he may not allow himself to physically pursue me again, that our first night may have been merely an impulse influenced by the drinks he'd had, not to be experienced again during my visit. But his polite, tender request revealed a yearning that still existed in him, without the assistance of alcohol. I sat contentedly beside him.

Together we listened to the diversity of languages spoken around us and observed the hipsters, as well as a hungry pigeon strutting what could pass for a professionally styled Mohawk. Being together was so easy. Laughter, amusement, the flow—our energy playfully caressed each other's before melding cohesively together. We were already one.

We remembered we'd wanted to play Ping-Pong during my visit. We recalled fondly the playfulness we'd engaged in during our match in Iguazú Falls, and we wanted to explore that opportunity again. Now seemed like the perfect time. We took a bus to a bar with a Ping-Pong table. It was occupied when we arrived, so we went for a walk to pass some time. We approached a busy intersection, and I boldly stepped into the street to cross. I'd looked for cars…but "the American way," not taking into account that the British drive on the opposite side of the road. Boris grabbed my arm.

"Wait!"

I knew I wasn't alone with this problem; the city had actually painted *Look Left* and *Look Right* at each intersection, which I learned to pay more attention to. I'd hoped to not stand out as a tourist, but I accepted my position with humility.

"Well, I'm not afraid to die, anyway. When it's my time, it's my time," I shared. "I tried to explain that to my parents," I continued. "They worry so much. I always tell them, well, what's the worst that can happen to me? I die, right? But I'm not afraid of that, because I believe the soul never dies, it simply occupies a different form. The release from one particular body is at the soul's choosing—the purpose for that life having already been accomplished—before it chooses to identify with another body and life experience. Therefore, how can I ever fear anything? And since everything comes from either fear or love, when we release fear from our experience, we always choose love."

"Wow." Boris paused a moment. "That's deep."

I smiled. I had barely touched the surface of the spiritual philosophy I so deeply wanted to share with him. My joy in having seen him grasp this concept that had been life-changing for me was softened by the realization that my time with him was so limited. There were many discussions and ideas I had waited so long to explore with him—knowing that they were best in person. And yet it takes time and appropriate opportunities to engage in-depth in those ideas. I had to appreciate and be grateful for these small ones I was given.

Our walk led us to a collection of food carts. Like Portland, London has an abundance of street food. Boris ordered an espresso, and I bought bubble tea. I was feeling playful, and bubble tea accentuated my mood. I recalled that first party I'd been to after moving to Portland; it was through a ridiculously enjoyable tapioca ball–spitting contest that I'd attracted my now good friend, Jean-Luc. Since that day, I can't miss an opportunity to shoot tapioca balls through a straw. I asked Boris to open his mouth and I demonstrated this favorite pastime of mine. Thankfully, he didn't choke.

We sat in the sun for the next half hour, me wearing his sunglasses, listening to him talk about needing to find more meaningful work. He was working for a betting company and did not feel right about helping people lose money. He preferred to work for a cause—preferably urban cycling or another community sustainability issue. He also shared with pride how friends back in Brazil had told him he'd been crazy to leave his job with a highly acclaimed American company, but he proved that the risk was worth it; he was so much happier in London.

It was at this time, quietly listening to him share pieces of his soul, that I realized I was falling in love with him. It was not a sudden or colossal shift—I had suspected I was already on my way even before arriving in London. I noticed how the pursuance of our dreams can actually make us more attractive; when we follow our bliss, our inner joy and spirit is reflected on a physical level as well. Boris appeared even more appealing to me than he had in Argentina.

He was engrossed in sharing his thoughts, often looking off into the distance, and I simply wanted to absorb his spirit. I saw the purity of his soul in his eyes. He was so beautiful. I feigned complete presence; I was listening, but my real focus was on exploring his essence. I decided wholeheartedly that I would not try to restrain those feelings. I wanted to love without fear, and I knew I could now do so without expectation or attachment to a particular result. I could simply love him. It was a priceless gift I could offer him.

We finished our drinks and returned to the bar to see if the Ping-Pong table had freed up. We found the players on their last game, so we purchased our paddles and took a seat while waiting for them to finish. Words were brewing inside of me; I'd literally been waiting years to tell him something. I'd known they needed to be said in person. It felt like an appropriate time to release the space they'd occupied inside me to the universe.

"I would like to share something personal with you," I began. I felt myself start to get nervous, as when I know I'm about to expose a sacred part of myself. He leaned forward; he could feel my energy shift into a vulnerable state for me.

"When I met you, I'd only ever been with one person, and it was not a pleasant experience for me. So I want you to know how special you were to me, and how much I trusted you, to be with you."

I stopped myself from adding any more history or detail. I'd said all I needed to say. I'd wanted not only to share the important role he'd played in my life but to release the shame I had previously felt for having been with just one person at the age of twenty-five.

Boris reached for my hand and held it. After a small pause, he replied, "I could sense something had happened in your past. I knew you were holding yourself back."

I paused before continuing, "I can tell *you* are also holding yourself back now. I understand your inner conflict regarding not wanting to hurt the woman you recently met. I want you to know that I would completely respect your decision if you decide not to pursue a sexual relationship with me. But I also want you to know that I've been aching to give myself to you in a way I wasn't ready to before. I want to be with you on a soul level. I'm ready to truly offer myself to you now."

I took a deep breath and sighed. *Ahhh, my truth was shared*. It felt like a toxic mass of energy had just poured out through my fingertips to disperse into the ether, laughing as it revealed to me its true form, *Ha ha ha...you thought I was real. I was just your silly imagination.* I allowed it to tease me before I continued, "You know, several of my friends back home joked that I wouldn't end up coming back from London." My eyes met Boris's. He was leaning back now, gazing at me as though he were searching for a deep truth.

The moment hung in silence.

"Is that a possibility?" he finally asked, with a traceable element of hope escaping from his eyes and his heart. I felt as though I were sinking into a warm bath. The romanticist in me wanted to scream, *Yes! Let's do this!* but my inner guidance replied, *No, not at this time.* I knew it wasn't the right time for me—for us. But oh, how sweet that would be, right? Like Celine in *Before Sunset*, quipping to Jesse how he was going to miss his plane.

Boris sighed deeply. "It's a complicated thing," he trailed off. I believed I already knew what he meant, but I wanted to hear it.

"What is?"

"You and me."

You and me. I liked the sound of that. Yet I had committed to nonattachment and managed to simply stay in the moment. What could I do with *now*? The future was unknown and irrelevant. Right now, I could love him. I could laugh with him. I could reach out and touch him, as I'd increasingly ached to do over the past few months—and even years before that. What pleasure! We were together. Right now. And that's all that mattered.

The energy shifted as the Ping-Pong table opened up.

"Let's go!" Boris stood, and we seized the table. The intensity of pensive emotion gave way to laughter as we resurrected our experience from Iguazú Falls and engaged in playful competition. I loved every moment; my body projected energetic enthusiasm for the game itself, but in reality my inner world was much more at play. I still couldn't believe I was there with him. My only regret was that the Ping-Pong table had to be between us.

Though I could have played much longer, there were others waiting for the table. We continued on our way, unsure of our next destination. Passing a French café that boasted of Nutella crepes, however, was enough to lead me there. We sat at a table by the window. The red vintage décor made me feel I was in Europe—even if the English don't consider themselves European. Our conversation switched to Spanish. My language skills had progressed a lot since we'd last seen each other. I could comfortably converse, and it felt so good to share that with him.

As I told him about my love for whales, what yoga meant to me, and books that greatly impacted my life, he fell into silence. His eyes took on a different cast. I knew it well. He'd looked at me this way as I arrived at Iguazú Falls and caught his gaze out the window of the bus. I am not in a position to call it love—that is a word he'd never used—but it was certainly loving. This time, rather than divert my gaze with fear, I played along. I did not acknowledge my awareness of his state of being but maintained my storytelling composure. I wanted to watch his intrigue play out naturally.

We took one more bus to the river. I'd wanted to cross Tower Bridge on foot. We'd so far had little physical contact throughout the day. I'd been craving touch but not initiating it. Walking across the bridge on this gray spring day, the wind from the river sent a chill our way; the moment felt magical. One particularly powerful breeze carried with it the seed of yearning. I could physically feel his energy reach for mine before his arms even did. He grabbed me and kissed me, and 100 percent of my body responded. He pulled away for us to continue our walk but kept his arm around my waist. Such joy, such connection.

It was time to take the tube home so I could get ready for the second night of the lindy exchange. I didn't want our day to end, but I felt called to follow through with my plans. The tube was quite full on that Saturday night. There were no empty seats, so we stood by the doors. Boris held the pole that I leaned my back against. My head touched his hand, and I felt him begin to stare at me. His fingers pulled away from the pole and began to grace my hair in a trepidatious way, as one would test the water before jumping in.

I glanced at him long enough to recognize "the look" again and then smiled and looked away. I wanted to offer him an opportunity to study me without being watched.

It had been six years. There was a lot of me I wanted him to discover. He knew I'd seen him, though.

"I'm not looking," he responded cautiously, like a child trying to convince a parent that he wasn't sticking his hand in the candy jar.

We arrived at our stop and rode the escalator to the exit in silence. He was one step below me; we felt another magnetic draw toward each other as he stepped up to kiss me. The background fell away. We weren't on a crowded escalator in a busy tube station. We were alone, together, at last.

AFTER A COUPLE of hours of swing dancing at Camden Centre, I took a break to eat a late dinner at a café. Raymond, a dancer I had known from Portland but who had moved to Germany a few years before, joined me. I'm always amazed at how small the world really is—especially the dance world, where people tend to travel a lot. We spent some time catching up; I told him about my job with Living Yoga. I clarified that though I practiced yoga, I didn't teach—my position was an office role.

"Why don't you teach?" he asked. I think he sensed my fear around the subject.

"Well, I'm rather afraid to be up in front of people." I admitted.

He looked at me as though he had something very important to say and wanted to be sure he had my attention. "Everything comes from either love or fear." He paused and then continued, "Have you ever heard of the series of books Conversations with God?"

The Universe is so fun.

"Oh, you have no idea!" I told him how I'd recently returned from a retreat with the author and how his books had so significantly shaped my life over the past six months—though of course, they'd really been quietly stirring within me over the past five years. Not to mention, I'd *just* said those words in my discussion with Boris earlier that day. (The Universe constantly speaks to us; the only question is are we listening.) I stored this conversation's message away for later; I knew there was something more to this teaching idea I needed to explore.

Though I wanted to stay and talk about spirituality all night, I had to rush and catch the last tube home.

"When will you be in Europe next?" Raymond asked as I said goodbye.

My face scrunched up as I thought of the expense of another trip of this distance. "I don't know…" I replied.

But he finished for me. "When you decide to, right?"

"Yes." I realized he was right. "When I decide to." Our minds have become so skilled at habitually cultivating excuses outside of ourselves for why we can't do something. In reality, it's simply a matter of deciding we are going to do it.

Raymond called after me as I hurried off, "I have two words of wisdom for you."

"What's that?"

"Inner stillness," he replied.

"I'll remember that," I called back and returned to the activity at hand: navigating London. Cultivating inner stillness within a large city can be difficult, but not impossible. I remembered struggling with it so intensely in

Buenos Aires. *We'll continue to be tested until we're no longer triggered,* I thought. This night on the tube, I smiled from my heart and took a deep breath. We get to choose what we bring our awareness to, just as we get to choose our reaction to any given stimuli. I chose, this night, to experience the chaos around me as just another perfect moment within my life's journey.

UPON EXITING THE tube and beginning the ten-minute walk to Boris's house, I heard my phone ring. It was Boris, of course—the only one who knew my local number.

"Hi!" I answered joyfully.

"Ahh. You had me so worried! I saw that you called, and I called back ten seconds later, and you didn't answer. I've been calling and texting you all night!"

Oops. I hadn't noticed. I was still unaccustomed to using this particular phone. I indeed had accidentally called him much earlier in the night.

"I'm so sorry! I'm fine—I'm almost home."

He sighed in relief, and I picked up my pace. For the second time during my visit, I received the best welcome-home greeting. He was in his bed, having stayed awake for me. He threw back the comforter and slid over to invite me in. I lay down alongside him, and he held me tenderly.

"Nice to see you."

I smiled at the commonness of his choice of words, as I knew they ran much deeper.

"It's good to have you back. If this were São Paulo, I would have called the police."

I laughed, though I knew he was serious. I actually felt grateful that I had mistakenly called him, because it led us to this moment. His concern was endearing; I felt taken care of. I used to have a hard time allowing myself to be nurtured; I thought it implied that I wasn't strong enough to take care of myself. I realized now that the greatest strength lied in surrender.

Boris began to touch me with great compassion and care and then reached for his phone and put on some blues music. Once again the sultry haze of B. B. King's guitar riffs filled the air between us. It was too much for both of us; our bodies burned to physically express the union of our souls with the music—and with each other. His arms encircled and explored my body, raising my shirt above my head and dropping it to the floor like a carelessly discarded candy wrapper. He could hardly wait to taste me, and I could hardly wait to be taken.

It was as the first time we made love—I allowed his movements to guide our experience. But this time I wasn't simply surviving, I was surrendering. I let myself go as we made unrestrained, unapologetic, beautiful love. I offered myself to him as I had in my recent dreams. And he took me in as one would take in the beauty of the season's first snowfall—with awe, inspiration, and disbelief. I was so grateful.

The intensity of our coming together was lightened when Boris reached down and took a long swig from the vodka bottle alongside his bed. My initial surprise gave way to laughter.

"Would you like some water?" he offered.

The bottle had been filled with water all along, Boris anticipating a perspiring night of lovemaking.

20
A Silent Teacher

DAY 3

Sunday began with a rush to get ready and meet up with colleagues from Boris's company for a picnic in Greenwich Park. The previous night had not offered either of us significant sleep, although when we did finally rise from bed, our faces, at least, exhibited a newfound glow. Everyone at the picnic was from a different country; I found pleasure in the fact that I was the only native English speaker in the group. Nearly five thousand miles from home, and I was the local-language "expert." We sat in a circle, chatted, dined, imbibed; Boris and a Brazilian friend played guitar; and I quietly took it all in. This was my first real exposure to who Boris was with his friends. He got progressively drunker throughout the long afternoon and evening, which I perceived as an opportunity to see how his personality evolved in such circumstances. Drunk Boris fathomed himself quite a comedian. He was more dramatic than usual and reveled in being the storyteller in the group.

Despite my being in my element while among people from all over the world, my introverted side was overtly present. I stayed in my inner space during the long afternoon, which meant that at times I had to step away from the group. I found a quiet spot about one hundred yards away where I could practice yoga. Even a year ago, I would have been too shy to practice in public. I knew I was being watched in the bustling park, but I was able to set that knowledge aside and retreat within myself and the moment. All I could see were the trees in front of me and the hill down below. I was so engaged in the practice, I didn't even hear Boris behind me, taking pictures as I moved through the poses. When I later saw the pictures, I realized he'd been there for a while. I conceded that he must have found those moments beautiful; he was inspired to leave his group of friends and quietly capture them.

I felt blessed. I'd offered another the experience of beauty—a connection to the Divine. I hoped I was an example that we all have this available to us. Returning to the group after my practice, I saw Jakub had turned his blanket to lie and face me. He too had shifted his source of entertainment away from the group and focused in on my movements.

"You're good," he stated with conviction. "You did all sorts of weird things."

Alex laughed at Jakub's professional opinion. "You're a real yoga expert, aren't you?"

I was just glad that another person was intrigued by yoga. Maybe he'd find it a useful tool for himself one day. I realized then that practicing yoga in public is actually the best place to practice. Like all things in life, what I do isn't about *me,* even though I must speak and act only to honor my own truth. It's about all those who are touched by what I do, who I am. If strangers can see me practice, and see the peace of my being, they will recognize what I was doing as one path to finding that peace and likely want that experience for themselves. What a great gift we can offer the world, simply by being ourselves. I realized then that I was already a teacher. We all are.

Evening gave way to night, and the picnic showed no sign of ending. I excused myself to take the bus home to get ready for that night's dance.

"Are you sure you can get home alright?" Boris asked as he followed me a few yards away. With the help of the map function on my phone, I said I felt confident.

"Okay, well, call me if you need anything or if you have any problem tonight."

I assured him I would, and he kissed me goodbye and went back to the group.

Feeling bad about how my missed phone call had made him worry the night before, I texted him when I arrived safely at the dance and attempted to call him later when I was headed back home. He did not answer the phone, but I figured he was probably just out where he couldn't hear it ring.

By the time I returned home after the dance, the house was dark and so quiet I didn't think anyone was home. Out of curiosity, I cracked open Boris's room, to surprisingly see his bent knee sticking out from the covers. The rest of him was buried in the blankets, out cold.

"So much for my emergency contact." I smiled. I was glad he'd made it home safe. I went back to my room, trusting we would both get a good sleep that night.

21
Mojo and Miracles

DAY 4

Monday was a bank holiday in the UK. I still don't really know what that means. I realize it's just a name for a federal holiday, but couldn't they have come up with a better name? In any case, I was grateful for the holiday, as it meant another leisurely morning with Boris. We made plans to meet up for dinner after the final dance of the exchange, an afternoon event, followed by what would be my inaugural visit to the Ain't Nothin' But blues bar. I'd heard so much about the bar, as Boris referred to it as his second home.

We had dinner at a lovely Italian restaurant near the bar; the conversation mostly revolved around the company he worked for, as he'd heard a reliable rumor that twenty people would be laid off the following day. Boris's heart and mind were heavy with the thought not that he might lose his job, but that colleagues with kids might lose theirs.

His somber mood distinctly lightened once we arrived at the blues bar. I understood instantly why this place was so special to Boris. I felt its magic too. It was a total dive bar; broken glasses decorated the floor of the women's restroom, and there was not enough toilet paper in either stall. But the energy was reminiscent of a large family gathering, complete with drunken Uncle John cheering too loudly at the corner stool and a woman I imagined as someone's mother-in-law dressed in an uncomfortably risqué fashion in the corner booth. But the music…oh, the music. It was their regular Monday night jam night, and though the rotating musicians had never played together before, they created melodies so moving that I didn't want to sit still. I was dying to dance.

"You know, there's a couple swing dancing near the bar," Boris relayed, having just returned with a drink.

"Really?!" I exclaimed. The place was so small and so packed that I had figured it wouldn't be appropriate to dance there, but making my way through the crowd, I located the couple, and dance they did.

People had cleared room a bit to enjoy the spectacle. I love how dancing lindy hop—and various other styles of dance—in public generates a magnetic attraction, drawing together everyone from the homeless man to the "cool" adolescent to the elderly lady reliving her youth. Dancing inspires people to ask themselves, "What if?" as they envision themselves being able to move as such free spirits and experience for themselves the joy they see on the dancers' faces. I waited until the song was over before eagerly approaching this couple.

"Are you here for the lindy exchange?" I asked.

"There was a lindy exchange here?" they asked, incredulously. It turned out they were visiting from France for just two days and had known nothing of the event that had drawn more than five hundred dancers from fourteen different countries to London for the weekend. I filled them in on what they'd missed and then asked permission from the woman to dance with her partner, whose name I learned was Fabien, before asking him.

Both responded with enthusiasm, and he and I waited for an appropriate tempo.

After some additional chatting and a lovely dance, I headed back to my seat alongside Boris. Perhaps twenty minutes later, Fabien returned, alone, and crouched down to talk to me. Boris, more of a proper gentleman than I a lady, offered him a seat beside me on the crowded bench. Squashed between an attractive young Frenchman on my left and an amorous Brazilian man on my right, I deliberated that life was quite good. A playful indication that the Universe is always participating in our lives did not escape my awareness as the band entered into Muddy Waters's "I Got My Mojo Working."

Fabien had asked me earlier how I knew Boris, whom I'd motioned as someone I was in town visiting. That's always a question that makes me smile a bit sheepishly, albeit enthusiastically, as I know the answer generates intrigue and youthful optimism. I think everyone likes to entertain the idea of the resurrection of an estranged international romance. Well, maybe not Fabien, in this particular case.

"We met in a hostel in Argentina, six years ago. We kept in touch, but we hadn't seen each other since." I realized now that he'd been trying to gauge if we were a couple—I had mistaken the woman he'd danced with as his girlfriend. He must have been satisfied with my answer, because now, sitting at our booth alongside Boris, he asked me what I was doing the following day. Boris played the gentleman again and assisted in trying to get our phones to be able to make international calls to each other, albeit to no avail. We made plans then and there instead, to meet at a tube stop at 11:00 a.m. the following day to explore Covent Garden. With arrangements confirmed, Boris and I said goodbye to "our" new friend and headed home.

Back home, we stopped in the kitchen for a drink of water before heading upstairs to bed.

"That French guy was really into you," Boris expressed.

"Nawww..." I disagreed, for argument's sake.

"Yes, he was! I saw the way he looked at you. He really liked you."

"Are you jealous?" I teased, lightly punching his arm.

"No," he replied with such authenticity and conviction that I knew it was the truth. What a shift from our dynamic in Argentina, when my dancing with another man had made him openly jealous. We'd both come a long way. We knew we had no right to deny each other opportunities of connection and relationship with those we met on our respective journeys. We simply wished for each other pure and unrestrained happiness.

I got in the comfortable habit of knowing that when I was in my room getting ready for bed each night, I would be visited by Boris. He would stand a bit awkwardly in my doorway, as there was nowhere to sit in the room other than the bed. I couldn't tell if he was looking for an invitation, either verbal or physical, to come in and sit on the bed or if standing was simply his preference. Eventually, we did always end up on the bed together—either in a reclined position or seated, as is what happened on this particular night. He had brought down a book from his room that a Spanish colleague, Iban Munárriz, had written, *Los Hijos de las Sombras.*

He described how it was a fantasy about a man who had lived in only his small Spanish town, but had spent countless hours in the library searching for clues as to what lay beyond their tiny village. Those who had ventured beyond the town's limits before him had disappeared, never to be heard from again. He knew there were inherent risks in undertaking such a journey, but it was a journey his soul was nonetheless called and determined to take.

Boris shared how the story moved him, as he could relate to the feeling of having been called to discover what else was "out there," and he had been deeply inspired by what the author had said in a video interview with a Spanish news station, after having won a literary award.

"Can I show you the interview?" he asked. I loved how he always asked if he could show me things. My answer was always a resounding, "Yes, of course!" I was delighted to discover things that moved him—whether it was a joke, a book, or any manner of belief.

The line in the interview of particular interest to Boris was in response to the question, "How does a man of the sciences come to be a writer of literature?" The author replied that having a degree in the sciences does not define who he is. He'd always been attracted to words and to literature, conceding that there can be many facets to one's personality. There was so much truth to his statement that it was easy for me to understand why Boris identified with it deeply. Our society, in particular, is so attached to asking, "What do you do?" and deciding who a person is based on that response. Wouldn't it be so much more interesting to ask, "What brings you joy?" or "What are your wildest dreams?" We'd certainly learn much more about a person.

I could see Boris was lost in thought. I imagined he was thinking of who he was—or wanted to be—outside of his job.

"You know, my ex-girlfriend once asked me, 'Who are you?' I responded with my job title. She said 'No, who *are* you? That's what you do.' I told her, 'I don't know. I'm a man.' She continued to argue, saying, 'That's your gender; that's not who you are.' I was getting frustrated by then. I didn't know who I was. I didn't get it."

I smiled patiently, albeit anxiously, waiting for him to finish. "Can I show you something?" It was my turn for show-and-tell. I picked up the notebook that was lying on the bed beside him and turned to a particular page.

"We did an exercise at the Conversations with God retreat I went to in March. We were asked to list ten endings to the statement, *I am.*" I showed him my list. "Then, we had to cross off three, then three more, then three more…until we were left with only one. We were to notice the ones that were hard for us to let go of as part of our identity. I was left with *I am love.* I knew that was the essence of all the others."

"Wow! I can't believe it," Boris exclaimed. "What are the chances of you having just done that exercise?" He marveled at the coincidence, but really, the Universe knows exactly what it's doing.

"There's one more thing I want to quickly show you," I said. I could see him getting tired, and he had to work the next day.

"I've been keeping a gratitude journal every day for the past couple of months." I fanned through the pages to show him the numerous lists. His mouth gaped open in astonishment.

"I read this book *Make Miracles in 40 Days: Turning What You Have into What You Want*. It teaches that when we consistently write down what we're grateful for, even when we're not feeling grateful—especially then, actually—miracles start to happen."

He was intrigued and nodded his head in agreement.

I continued, "Announcing gratitude for things you want, as if you already have them, is a powerful tool for manifesting your desires. We're even to write specific things we're *not* feeling grateful for—without trying to figure out why we could be grateful for them. Simply writing them down in a spirit of gratitude shifts the energy around it. For example, look—I wrote, *My debt! Yay! Woohoo!* almost every day."

His eyes scanned the rest of my list. I let him read the page, but then I turned a little embarrassed. "Well, you're actually on some of these lists."

He remained silent for a few moments. Then, he moved closer to me on the bed and hugged me. One of those hugs that sends radiance through every pore of your body. It said, *Thank you* in a much more beautiful way than words can alone. I have learned that words are the least effective form of communication, as they can easily be misconstrued. Feelings, however, are a great transmitter of truth. I received his energy and could easily interpret it as gratitude. My gratitude for him had been met with his own gratitude—for me, or for my appreciation for him, I wasn't sure. But it didn't matter.

I realized later that this day marked day forty in my gratitude journal. I would say a miracle was certainly being made.

Boris held my face in his hands and kissed my lips. "Goodnight" he said quietly and went upstairs to bed.

22
Feeling the Blues

DAY 5

Tuesday was my first day to explore London independently. I had planned to meet up with Fabien at 11:00 a.m., but when my alarm went off at 9:00 a.m., I knew the effort would be futile. My body had still not adjusted to the eight-hour time difference, and mornings were tough. Though I felt bad for breaking my commitment, part of me was relieved. I had a lot to process and take in.

I decided to visit Covent Garden anyway. The tourist-centric market with overpriced swag and boutique shops, however, was of little interest to me. I quickly continued on. I hadn't intended to walk quite so far, but my habit while traveling is to look at a map and say, "Oh, the next item of interest is only half a mile further." After doing this repeatedly, I end up walking several miles beyond my original intention, only to realize, at the point when I start to get tired, that now I have to walk the whole way back. Thankfully, London has plenty of conveniently located tube stops. I covered all of St. James Park and Hyde Park before taking the nearest tube back to Boris's place. On the walk from the tube stop to his house, I received a text that he'd just gotten off the tube and was walking home.

"Me too!" I texted back, expecting to see him approaching from behind at any time. Arriving at the house, I set my things down and went to the sink for some water.

I made a concerted effort to look for him through the window, still thinking he'd be coming any moment. I eventually put down my glass and turned, only to see him sitting in a chair against the opposite wall, watching me.

"Ahhh!" I laughed. "Were you going to say anything?!" I felt vulnerable, having been unknowingly watched, but at the same time safe. I walked over and sat across his lap, as would a child. It was so natural for me to want to be pressed up against his body.

He remained quiet. The layoffs they'd heard rumored had taken place, and he was feeling a heavy burden of responsibility for his friends who'd lost their jobs while he kept his. He also felt so disgusted with the company that he was contemplating quitting the next day—both so he could focus on finding a new job for himself and also to perhaps spare one of his colleagues from being laid off.

His eyes were dark and troubled, his spirit sagging. I was sad to see him suffer, but grateful for the opportunity to be there for him. I fought the urge to tell him that he could move away from suffering simply by changing his reaction to the events that occurred. I understood that there's a time and a place for grieving, and this was one of those times. I stayed with him as he remained in his dark place.

As was his practice when feeling down, he grabbed his guitar, pulled out his phone, and began playing along to blues music. He shared some songs with me that he was hoping to play in a blues band he was trying to form. One was "Stormy Monday," which we'd heard at the blues jam the night before. I asked if he'd ever heard Eva

Cassidy's version—my favorite. He had not heard of her, so I ran upstairs to get my iPod. He brought down his split headphones—an invention I was not even aware of and couldn't fathom too many people having the opportunity to use, though I was eager for this chance to use them with Boris.

Together we sat, for at least the next hour, experiencing blues songs together. Eva Cassidy lulled us to darker depths with "Stormy Monday" while Nina Simone teased us further into despair only to raise us back with "Ain't Got No Home."

I knew even then that the moment was precious; it felt like a scene from a movie. There was something overtly intimate about listening to music through headphones together. It was like escaping into a private world in which we revealed our deepest secrets to each other. When his roommate Jakub arrived home and called out, "Hey guys!" I felt as though we'd been caught in the act of making love. I believe Jakub felt the energy, as he quickly made his way upstairs, despite our warm hellos in return.

The energy had been interrupted, and we soon shifted gears as Boris began exploring the job market online and making a call to a colleague, who happened to also be from Brazil. Listening to him speak rapid Portuguese was a pleasure. I could make sense of some words due to its proximity to Spanish, but for the most part, it just felt like an enchanting melody. I'm not sure if that was because it was Portuguese, or because it was *him* speaking Portuguese. I think it was the latter.

Jakub eventually joined Boris and me in the living room, where we engaged in our own activities for the next couple of hours. I had taken up journal writing again since the Conversations with God retreat, and sat reflecting on what my experience in London might have to teach me, while Boris and Jakub busily typed away at their computers. I felt like part of the home's funny little family. I settled in with ease.

23
You're Better Now

DAY 6

Wednesday I decided to explore Notting Hill—mainly because my guidebook told me there was a café and grocery store there called Planet Organic. I was in seventh heaven in the shop; I recognized many comfort products of mine from the United States but also some local products that gave me great excitement and joy—namely handmade raw chocolate. I stocked up—mostly for gifts, but I knew my own palate would experience the pleasure of their charms as well. I also happened to walk by the Indian restaurant that the airport taxi driver had recommended as his favorite in London. I took it as a sign and texted Boris the suggestion of meeting there for dinner.

Boris had a way of sneaking up on me as I waited outside restaurants for him. Without a word, he would come up beside me and sweep me along with him like the wind collecting a particle of dust. This time, however, my heavy bag made me impossible to move.

"How can you carry that thing?" he questioned. It would not be the last time he stood in astonishment at the weight of my baggage.

The dinner was fantastic. I'd been told the Indian food in London was the crème de la crème, and I wholeheartedly agreed. The conversation, likewise, was rich and inspirational. Boris was still troubled about his company's situation and, it seemed, the state of the world. There had been several incidences during my visit he shared with exasperation and a touch of anger; often he'd read news of a horrible crime—usually in his home town in Brazil. I'd listen with compassion, but not until that night at dinner did I open up with my thoughts.

"I hear you that that's a horrible thing that happened. But can I tell you why that doesn't make me angry or depressed?" One of the things I learned about Boris during this trip—or perhaps relearned—is that he was open to hearing anything. Nothing made him uncomfortable or made me feel judged, and therefore I was comfortable sharing anything with him. This was such a great gift. Can you imagine if we could communicate with everyone in this transparent way?

"It's hard to articulate in few words, because it's part of a much larger context, but I'll do my best. Basically, I believe that souls inhabit specific bodies by their own choice. There is a particular experience they are seeking in this chosen lifetime. It could be that the soul wants to experience what it means to be forgiveness, but in order for it to know forgiveness, someone has to do something to it that requires it to forgive.

"Therefore, the rape victim in Brazil is offered the choice to view herself as a victim, or she can choose to rise above the experience to perhaps use it as a means to help ensure that such violence doesn't happen again. Maybe it's her soul's purpose to become a speaker or therapist who will help countless others. If she were to die as a result of the crime, perhaps her mother is inspired to work toward peace on her child's behalf—or even a complete stranger who heard the story on the news. We are always cocreating our experience, so we never know the ripple effect particular occurrences will have. One who is violated is always offered the choice to consider, 'What hurts this person so bad that they feel they have to hurt me to heal it?' We can decide to be hurt by something someone has done or said to us...until we decide *not* to be."

I could see he was still engaged, so I continued,

"As for the violators themselves, it's important to remember that the soul always chooses the quickest path to achieve its purpose. Perhaps their purpose is to experience their lowest low, that they may face themselves and realize who they are *not*. The Universe operates by a divine dichotomy; in the absence of what we are not, we cannot know what we *are*. We can't know hot if we don't know cold—there would be no point of reference in which to 'know' anything. We have to experience it. So, 'evil' has to exist—which is really just a subcategory of fear—in order to know and experience love.

"It's often our instinct to fight violence with more violence, but history has shown that this doesn't work. When we view the incidents and outcomes in life from a 'what works versus what doesn't work' paradigm, rather than 'right versus wrong,' we see that if our ultimate goal is peace, we will not get there by inflicting more violence or subjugating others with laws and limitations. We have to send love to our perpetrators—reacting with hate only continues the cycle."

I took a deep breath. I get so passionate about this topic that I can end up rambling. But he'd stayed with me.

"It sounds like Allan Kardec's philosophy of Spiritism," Boris offered. "It's very popular in Brazil." I was pleasantly surprised that my explanation was not met with disbelief or criticism. He seemed open to considering the idea. I remembered how adamantly he'd identified as an atheist when we'd first met and how, even now, he cringed at the word *God*. But if we replace *God* with another, less triggering name, it can become a lot easier to open up a dialogue with others on the same topic.

"Hmm. I've never heard of him," I admitted. "Of course, these ideas have existed for centuries. The teachers that I've had are just a few messengers of many and their books just a few tools to reach the same place. Some people may identify and connect with different messengers—none are right or wrong. And, of course, even if in the end we find out that what we believed in our lifetime isn't so, I still cannot think of a better way to live. These beliefs have brought me inner peace and tremendous joy—and when one person experiences peace and joy, the whole world benefits from its expression."

Boris fell silent and gazed off into the distance. I offered a few moments of silence before allowing myself to inquire, "What are you thinking?"

He looked at me affectionately before answering, "I was wondering when I would see you next."

We allowed the words to trail off into the distance. We didn't have an answer, nor did we need one. We were here, now.

I could have sat and discussed philosophy for the next several hours, but Boris was getting anxious to get the bill and get home. We'd talked casually about me teaching him some basic yoga poses, and back at home I was surprised when he came into my room and said, "Ready?"

I started by teaching him breath work, for as I'd been taught, "if you're not connecting the breath to the movement, you're not doing yoga—you're simply stretching." After just fifteen minutes of focused breathing and basic poses and stretches, we sat on the bed together.

"Thank you. I feel better."

I could see a visible difference in his expression; his face was more relaxed and his energy more open. I was so grateful for the opportunity to share this tool with him.

As often happens when the body relaxes and the mind quiets, intimacy—of both the emotional and the physical kind—naturally flows and reaches new heights. Our bodies, already next to each other, hypnotically reached for the other. What ensued was another beautiful night of making love.

At one point, our bodies joined in a seated position. His eyes caught our shadow on the wall. He moved the comforter for a better view and raised my body up, drawing my attention to the moving image.

"Look at us," he said softly. "We are together. It's so beautiful."

I nearly cried. Could there be a more divine expression of love?

Moving into a reclined position, he whispered in my ear,

"Why did you wait so long?" They were words his body called out, not his mind. Our minds could articulate why six years had passed without seeing each other. But it was as if our bodies wanted an explanation, and it better be a damn good one.

Several minutes passed.

"You're better now," he stated. I think he was answering his own question. The Universe had us wait so long, so that we could come together again in this particular way, at this particular moment. We were ready for each other now—not before. We sank into each other more, before finally relaxing into a shared release.

I took in the expression on his face with a slight chuckle. "You always look so surprised when you cum," I smiled.

"That's because it was so fucking amazing," he said with bewilderment. "When I'm with you, the whole background disappears." He gazed up at the ceiling and moved his arms in the manner of a magician.

Talk about making a girl feel special.

Woman. I corrected myself. I was a woman now. At the age of thirty-one, I finally allowed myself that distinction. It was about time.

24
A Three-Minute Love

DAY 7

With Boris at work the next day, I explored more neighborhoods independently. I made a stop at Foyle's, an independent bookstore, to pick up a copy of Napoleon Hill's *Outwitting the Devil* as a gift for Boris. I felt it was very appropriate at this transitional time in his life and career. Just as the books of Conversations with God are written as a personal dialogue with God, *Outwitting the Devil* is a personal dialogue with the devil, revealing how the "devil" uses fear, procrastination, anger, and jealousy to prevent us from realizing our personal goals as well as revealing the principles of good that can allow us to overcome unhelpful ways and find success in life. I figured Boris would be more open to a dialogue with the devil than one with God.

After another day of walking, I felt myself getting cranky. I realized with some self-analysis that, as is often the case when we're removed from joy, it was simply my body telling me that its basic needs weren't being met. I was tired and hungry. After attempting unsuccessfully to find a local café with comfortable indoor seating, I finally gave up and accepted the nearest option—Starbucks. I'd traveled all the way to London and ended up at a Starbucks. I gave myself permission to not feel guilty, on the basis of needing to listen to my body's needs over my mind's insistence of what a "real" traveler would do. In truth, I was still experiencing local culture—Starbucks was a part of London's contemporary culture now too.

Indulging in a delightful cup of tea and a snack, I rebalanced. Boris soon called to tell me he'd gotten out of work early and was able to meet me for dinner before the blues dance lesson he'd agreed to attend.

Alex met Boris and me at the dance venue the Tattershall Castle, which was actually a boat. I watched as Boris and Alex participated in the beginner lesson. I was so grateful for the opportunity to expose others to blues dancing, as it had been such an important outlet for me over the years. The joining of body, mind, and spirit in connection with another, in response to a style of music that for me—and I knew for Boris, as well—evokes such passion and pleasure. A good blues dance looks and feels like making love. NPR even did a special on it called "The Healing Power of Blues Dancing" that describes the experience so beautifully. Often without even knowing the other's name, two bodies can communicate a significant history of intimacy and attraction. Time and again, I've heard blues dancers share stories about having had their lives transformed by this feeling of intimate connection—to a partner and to their own body—that the dance offers them. Blues music has, for many, saved them.

I am incredibly intrigued by the correlation between blues music and spirituality. I had once heard that blues music had been called devil's music because it can generate a sacred consciousness that posed a threat to traditional religion. In the past, people looked to religion as the primary outlet for relief from suffering. Blues music and dancing provided an alternative to the church and, therefore, a perceived loss of control.

I found great pleasure in seeing Boris engage and connect with the dance and gain confidence using his body as an expression of what he was experiencing from the music. Dance, if we allow it to be, is really a physical expression of our personality, our sensuality, and our soul. When we draw from that energy, we are able to cross boundaries with another human being—our dance partner—in a vulnerable but safe way. It's an opportunity to practice falling in love without expectation or attachment. Your partner simply asks that you show up authentically and share your spirit—for three minutes only. For the physically inhibited, there is no awkward moment of questioning, "How long do I hold this hug?" The answer in dance is always simply, "Until the music stops."

It's amazing, however, how many relationships end up being born from those three minutes. Once we give others permission to touch us, to hold us, to truly know us, our own humanity and our place within the larger human race begins to meld together. We realize we are already one. Our soul cries out for more, and we feel more confident asking for it. It's really a meditation. There are few other times that everything else in my world falls away. Dancing gets me there instantly.

We brought the spirit of the dance back to Boris's place that night. After getting ready for bed and dimming the lights in his bedroom, Boris began to play guitar. I was changing out of my clothes, about to put on my nightshirt, when the music stopped me. I wanted to dance—

right there, in the nude, by myself. I never used to like dancing by myself—in front of other people, that is. But I felt inspired. I felt beautifully vulnerable, and I wanted to play with that feeling.

I remembered a blues dance workshop I'd taken years before, when the instructor shared a concept that I found really powerful:

"Energy never stops. Let it flow. When you feel momentum in your arm, let it extend out to your hands, your fingers...*use* it. Where do you want to take it?"

It's like playing tennis or baseball. Coaches say to allow the racket or bat to follow through. Yet how many times in life do we physically stop or hold back our energy? We fight our impulses to reach out and touch another, because we're afraid of...what? We refrain from raising our arms in the air when standing at the ocean; we want to express the power of what we're taking in, but we're afraid people will think we look like a fool. We allow children to playfully run around the beach and roll in the sand; we admire them with envy, because they can engage in this behavior because they're kids...but why can't we? Why do we always hold back?

I allowed my energy to flow that night. I felt it extend throughout my fingertips; I never stopped it—I simply redirected it. I could collect it outside of my body and bring it back within my body. We think we're simply bodies housing energy, but we're actually housed *by* energy. It's all around us, available to us, to play with.

The moment made Boris recall our night at the hostel together in Buenos Aires, drinking wine and dancing in our locked dorm room.

"I need to thank Marco," he began.

"What for?" I smiled. I knew why.

"For leaving me alone with you that night."

Thank you, Marco. God bless you.

25
Reality Hits You Hard, Bro

DAY 8

Boris and I decided to take a day trip together that Friday. Cambridge wasn't Paris, but that's because Paris wasn't meant to be. After some delays on the tube, we took a cab the last half mile, and even then we barely made our train. I recalled other times in my life when this situation would have greatly stressed me out. This time around, I just kept telling myself that everything was perfect. As I've learned to say at the sign of adversity, "This problem has already been solved for me."

We were meant to catch that train, and we immediately relaxed into the hour ride. Boris used the time to prepare for a phone interview for a new job he had soon after we arrived. I used the time to gaze out at the English countryside. I felt like I could be back in my home state once again. The landscape was relatively flat, with open fields of grass and the occasional stunning field of wildflowers emanating an incandescent yellow glow. Upon looking up from his work, Boris would eagerly reach for his camera to capture the passing natural splendor. As he returned to his studies across from me, I was able to watch him without his noticing, an opportunity to take him all in. It was my turn to indulge in moments of childlike captivation.

We had made no plan for our day in the college town. We'd done no research on attractions, history, or events.

Sometimes the best trips are the ones we sit back and spontaneously let plan themselves.

Before exploring, however, we needed to find a quiet café so Boris could have his 10:00 a.m. interview. We ended up at the delightful Café Julienne for the next hour. Boris sat down on the cushioned bench at a small round table. I sat down at the next table over. I'd wanted to give him some space to focus on his interview.

After a few minutes with this arrangement, however, Boris turned to me with the slightest hint of disappointment in my choice. "Sit here," and motioned next to him. I was touched; even while in an important interview, he did not need space from me.

I patiently waited for the conclusion of the interview. After about twenty minutes, I put down my magazine and took a deep breath. I am accustomed to breathing deeply in a way that some people interpret as exasperation, but I'm actually relaxing more into the moment. I'm not sure what Boris's interpretation was, but he reached out and held my hand. If he felt I would have preferred to be out seeing the sights of Cambridge, he would have been wrong. I preferred to be right where I was—with him—participating in his journey. I thought of the quote attributed to John Lennon, "Life is what's happening while you're busy making plans." This was life.

Soon afterward, we rose to leave the café and discover what our day would present. We ended up taking a sightseeing bus tour of the city, which included a stopover punting excursion (think Venice gondola ride but with a lot less flair). We each wore headphones to listen to the history of the sites we passed along the way. My playfulness sparked when I realized you could choose a language by selecting various stations. When Boris wasn't looking, I took the liberty of switching his to French. The look on his face was priceless. It took him a moment to process what had happened.

"Hey!" he laughed.

My inner nymph giggled in delight. Those are the moments when my spirit feels most free.

Though the history was fascinating to consider, the real beauty of the day came from simply being together in an environment that was new to both of us. We sat on the upper deck of the bus. It was a gray day; the wind was strong and cold, but I loved how it made me feel alive. Boris went to great lengths to cover me with his spare jacket, and I settled into his warm embrace. I remembered sitting next to him on a wooden tourist train in Iguazú Falls. Here we were together again as tourists. It had been six years; I felt like a different person, and aspects of him were significantly different as well, but somehow his spirit had preserved the same mesmeric quality I could not have escaped had I wanted to try. No individual being on this earth is more special than another, I knew, but I recognized that he would regardless always hold a special place in my heart.

I reveled in another intimate encounter when it came time for our punting trip. Though we had an excellent guide—an obvious history buff who excelled in comedic storytelling—my attention was more on the subtleties of touch and connection with Boris. Beneath a shared blanket at one end of the boat, I laid against his chest in the tuck of his arm. He rested his head upon mine, and I took great pleasure in feeling the cushion of his cheek upon my forehead. I wondered if he was feeling the exchange of energy that I was feeling.

Our boat continued leisurely along, trailed by a flock of ducks obviously accustomed to receiving the occasional handout from amused passersby. Every now and then another punting boat rowed up alongside us, and we marveled at the ability of the drivers to maneuver their long wooden crafts beneath the narrow bridges that crossed over the river. I half expected to end up either in the river or within the other boat, but rather than fear a collision, I flirted with the possibility of an adventure. Alongside the river banks, wildflowers of every color marked the arrival of spring. Willow trees occasionally extended their melancholy tresses over our heads, seeming to mourn our passing. I had my own experience of mourning—I'd have preferred to stay infinitely beneath the private sanctuary their natural cloak provided, with Boris by my side.

I wondered what Boris was thinking as we glided along the river, but I didn't want to interrupt the sacredness of the moment to ask out loud—especially when it was merely a curiosity of the ego that desired an answer. I was content to simply have my own experience. I trusted that the moment was precious to him, too.

The punting excursion ended all too quickly, and we reboarded the bus to finish the rest of the sightseeing tour. At its conclusion, we both noticed our appetites. We stopped for lunch at a sushi restaurant and then checked the map for directions to the final two places we knew we had to visit: a chocolate shop for me and an English pub called the Blind Pig for Boris. Convinced we were headed in the right direction, we could now walk peacefully along and take in the sights and sounds of this delightful college town. Or so I thought. I remember laughing boisterously at something while stepping down into the street, when I was shaken out of my blissful state by a bicyclist coming up behind me shouting, "Get out of the fucking street, you idiot!"

Ooops.

"Sorry!" I attempted, but he was already long past me. I forgot, once again, that traffic—bicycles included—would not be coming at me along the left side of the street. I felt the natural tendency to react with hurt or anger at his words, but I knew I had the choice of allowing the incident to impact my day—or even my moment—in a negative way, and I didn't see any benefit to that.

I'll choose to see it with humor instead, I thought. I mean really, is it even possible to hear *fucking* said with a British accent and not find it humorous? The choice was really that simple. Of course, the ego will often try to interfere with, *Hey! He was rude!* or *He's right. I* am *an idiot.* But in any case, we are in control of our experiences, and I wanted to return to the state of bliss I'd been in before the interruption. If we practice this freedom of choice regularly, it gets easier and easier, to the point where it is second nature. Therefore, all of these people who challenge us, or seemingly wrong us, are actually our greatest teachers. For how can we practice being peace without experiencing adversity?

We made it to the chocolate shop—a natural pick-me-up for me, had I still needed one. I derived great pleasure from picking out fifteen various truffles. The experience triggered a memory of my first time ordering ice cream in Argentina. "I would like a small cup of chocolate ice cream, please," I ordered in Spanish.

"And? What other flavor?"

Wait, you mean I get *two* flavors? Sweet! "And strawberry."

"And?" he replied again.

What? This was incredible! *Three* flavors, when ordering only one cup?

"And *dulce de leche*!" My enthusiasm soared as I struggled to maintain my composure. I had no idea what I'd been missing out on in the United States. *This* was a cultural tradition we needed to adopt.

Now, I again felt like a queen without limitation as I watched the shopkeeper delicately place truffle after truffle inside a boutique box. He then wrapped the box up nicely with a Tiffany-blue ribbon for me to bring back home, but I knew the elegant packaging wouldn't last past the train ride.

With a childlike smile on my face and an extra spring in my step, I headed out the door with Boris, onward to his stop. Upon arriving at the pub, agreeing with the vibe and taking in the selection of beers, his energy shifted to that of pure delight—he was practically giddy.

"You're so happy!"

"Ha-ha, yeah. I am!" He agreed, carrying his beer back to the table. Beer was to him what sweets were to me. We both were on cloud nine.

We left the pub and waited for a bus that would bring us to the train station. We had thought it the most efficient means of getting there, but the driver thought otherwise. With a look of disbelief, he scolded, "You want to take the bus to the train station in *this* traffic?" He threw his hands up incredulously. "You're better off walking!"

"Only in England would a driver refuse to take our money," Boris noted with amusement.

We made our way back to the train station by foot and settled into a booth in what was then an empty car. This time we sat next to each other. The day had brought us closer together. I cracked open the box of truffles that had been beckoning me for the past hour.

"You really love chocolate, don't you?" he marveled.

"Yes, I do! Did you know that chocolate triggers the same endorphins a woman feels while orgasming?" I replied.

He did not, but the suggestion made his eyes travel down the length of my body, at which point I accidentally dropped crumbs of chocolate all down my light blue dress. Boris jumped to get hand soap from his bag (ever the prepared traveler), and I began brushing the brown flecks from my chest.

"You missed some here"—he lightly touched my inner thigh—"and here...and here." He tenderly touched various parts of my body in a playfully intimate way. My body warmed. All it ever took was the slightest touch from him for my body to respond with a craving that rivaled my passion for chocolate.

I smiled, and he withdrew his hand, as if he were now somewhat embarrassed by his suggestive gesture.

"I'm saving some chocolates for your roommates, to thank them for letting me stay at your place for so long." I paused before continuing, "How can I thank you, as well?"

Boris looked at me sweetly. "You've done enough. How can I thank you for coming?"

I kissed his cheek and agreed, "You've done enough."

They were words that didn't really need to be spoken. The way we looked at each other was clearly representative of our shared appreciation. But sometimes words are still pleasant to hear.

After a few moments of silence, Boris asked the question we'd left hanging a couple of nights before at the Indian restaurant: "When will I see you next?"

It was the ever-present elephant in the room. I had to make a consistent choice not to ask myself, *What happens next?* To be fully present and enjoy all of the charm this experience had to offer, I needed to approach each moment without expectation. Nonetheless, I knew it was not really a question, but a statement of admiration for how special our time was together.

I later wished I would have replied with a variation on the line that Raymond had suggested upon asking me when I'd next be in Europe: *When we decide to.* Instead, after some quiet sighs that weren't answers at all, Boris and I got lost in conversation. His job was still heavy on his mind, and he started sharing an idea he had for how one of the betting games he was developing could actually raise money for a charity. The idea was brilliant and creative, and I fell a little deeper in love with his mind and spirit.

Settling into home that night, my body retaliated at the idea of getting ready to go out again. Boris had already left to attend another of Jakub's band's gigs. I had planned to attend a dance event, but I knew as soon as I sat down that it was going to be a relaxing night in for me. I needed some "introvert time." I sent some e-mails off to friends—many were eager to hear status updates on my little love affair—wrote in my journal, and read. I was just about to go to sleep when I received a text from Boris, asking if I was still awake. Jakub had forgotten his key, and Boris was about to give him his so he could head home to bed and Jakub could remain at the show longer. As all things in this great Universe, nothing happens by accident—including Jakub forgetting his key so that I'd have to wait up for Boris. What I was treated to was a side to Boris I had not seen before—a side that became one of my favorites.

When I heard the knock on the door, I went downstairs and let him in. A storm of energy flew in, to complement the rainstorm outside. Soaking wet and out of breath, having run so as not to keep me up too late, he huffed, "I'm going to shower and change—I'll be right back!" as he rushed up the stairs. I went up to bed, not sure I'd be awake by the time he got out. He was fast though, and came back down to my room and stood in the doorway with a very serious expression on his face.

"Reality hits you hard, bro," he declared.

What is he talking about? I thought.

He showed me his upper arm, which had a baseball-size bruise on it, the result of running into a pole while blues dancing on the boat. He survived several years of practicing martial arts without a scratch, but after one night of blues dancing, he was already injured.

I acknowledged that I didn't understand his bro reference, so he excitedly jumped into show-and-tell mode. Pulling out his phone, he lay down in bed beside me and showed me a video that had gone viral. However, the part that made me laugh until I had tears in my eyes (and still does every time I think of it) was Boris's reaction to the video. He had all the words, nuances, and onomatopoeia memorized and could act it out with great enthusiasm. He sat up cross-legged in my bed, looking like a little boy but for being shirtless and revealing the strong body of a man. He bounced and sang gleefully—with an adorable Portuguese accent, of course.

"Who is this crazy Brazilian man in my bed?" I laughed out loud. I did not recognize him, but I loved him! I was exhausted and in great need of sleep, but I couldn't get enough of this guy. He proceeded to show me two more videos of the same nature and acted those out as well.

A side effect of exhaustion for me is extreme goofiness. I was not the one being goofy this time, but his enthusiasm was contagious. My side hurt, but I couldn't stop laughing. By now, he'd finished his routine and had begun calming down, but I still had a severe case of the giggles.

"What are you laughing at?" he asked. He sincerely had no idea.

I just continued to laugh, crying, "I'm sorry" between gasps of air.

"Laughter is good," he replied and just smiled at me in awe, wondering what came over me.

Finally, we were both calm and being called to sleep. He stayed in my bed that night. Could there have been a more perfect ending to a perfect day? Well, every day is perfect, but I would say this one was pure bliss.

26
Dance so Someone Watches

DAY 9

Saturday morning came too soon and presented me with an opportunity to notice when I wasn't being my highest self. We began to make love that morning, but external circumstances interfered (to spare Boris's reputation, I want to clarify that it was not of the performance variety). After a few attempts, Boris stopped and leaned back, staring at the ceiling.

"Are you okay?" I asked, not sure why he had stopped.

"I'm thinking too much," he replied. I assumed it was about the woman he had met. He finally shared that he thought perhaps the interferences were signs that this wasn't right, at least not now.

"It has nothing to do with you," he reassured. "You're perfect." He stroked my stomach.

It's amazing how our minds can latch on to only one part of a story. What I heard was, *I'm ashamed to be with you,* which was not even close to what he'd expressed. He went on to explain that another interference was his roommate being in the hallway. I allowed the comment to manifest into perceived shame of my presence, thinking, *I've spent too many years ridding myself of shame around sex to still have it enter my bedroom.* I was caught up in the fantasy—the fantasy that I was somehow wronged. I got out of bed and dressed and hurried to get ready for a dance workshop I'd signed up for.

We walked out of the house together in silence—he needed to visit the grocery store that was on my route. After parting ways, it didn't take more than fifteen minutes alone for me to realize, *Oh, man. I was* not *love just there!* I'd asked him to be vulnerable with me and then didn't create a safe space for it, because of my own lapse into insecurity. No matter what he'd said, if it was his truth, I needed to respond with love. Redo, please? I sent him a text saying I understood and told him to have fun at the party he would be at the rest of the day. That's all I could do for now.

That night I worked to center myself back home. The housemates were all at a party, so I took the opportunity to prepare a Thai dinner for the following night. It was the only meal I would cook in London; it felt good to be in the kitchen. Between cooking and cleaning, I joyfully danced around the kitchen. I had put on some blues music. Etta James was belting "I'd Rather Go Blind," and I felt inspired to join in. It was then that I noticed an older man walking slowly outside the kitchen window, taking it all in.

I could have become embarrassed and stopped dancing, but I decided not to. They say to dance like no one's watching, but I say to dance so someone watches, so that someone else may feed off your joy and spirit and perhaps be inspired to dance as well—or at the very least, smile. I smiled at the man, as if to say, "It's okay if you watch," and continued letting fly my creative impulses. It was an everyday moment of ecstasy, and it was mine to seize.

27
Chocolate or Sex? Sex, Please.

Day 10

My trip was winding down. I had known it would go fast. Sunday was the last full day Boris and I would spend together, as he'd have to work the next day. There was a job fair he planned to attend at Brick Lane near Old Spitalfields Market, which was where I was headed to do some last-minute gift shopping for friends and family. Strolling down the street where we'd spent our first full day together, I already tasted a touch of bittersweetness. Amid the plethora of ethnic food stalls that lined the street, our palates were drawn to an Argentinean empanada stand. We never could turn those down. Together we indulged in savory tomatoes and cheeses encrusted in delectable fried dough.

Boris continued to the job fair and I to the market. I bought several beautiful pieces of art, including a framed photograph of a Spitalfields building, with *Today's going to be a good day...* painted above the door. I knew I'd remember Spitalfields as the "bookend" setting of this incredible trip. I hoped the precious details of each day would forever be imprinted in my memory.

A couple of hours passed before we met up for lunch in another food market and then walked to catch the tube to return to the Ain't Nothin' But blues bar. I'd been looking forward to returning since the night we'd first gone there. We boarded the tube and stood near one of the sliding doors. Boris stood holding the hand rail above and I the pole. The steady motion of the train gave our bodies a gentle sway. Without words or even looking directly at each other, we communicated by accentuating the rocking of our bodies. Back and forth they swayed until they touched, then fell away and returned to each other again. It was a beautiful moment of sensual play, a private exchange on a crowded train.

The intimacy of those moments brought to fruition a more physical exchange. Riding up the escalator after exiting the train, Boris reached to kiss me in a manner that made my heart stop.

"You're such a good kisser," I confessed.

"You inspire me."

We made our way out from the underground and back into a shared world, beyond where simply the two of us existed.

IT WAS ANOTHER jam night at the blues bar. We enjoyed affectionately giving nicknames to the players we were coming to know, such as Grumpy Cat, for the highly talented guitarist who never cracked a smile.

"He looks like he was just woken up and forced to be here," Boris joked.

After multiple incredible, moving jams, a new group, led by the emcee of the night and including our favorite guitarist, took my experience to a new level. All I could say repeatedly throughout the set at its highest moments was, *"Fuck!"* I otherwise completely lacked the vocabulary to depict the moment. I looked at Boris; he was having the same experience. It was beyond experiential in the physical realm—it was transcendental.

Such powerful experiences are not new to me, but they don't happen with great frequency. The majority of the times that I've felt so deeply moved have been in response to music. Music is a mighty tool for me.

Boris read my mind. "I'd rather be blind than deaf," he shared. I agreed.

As the song finished, I looked around the room.

"Do you think any of these other people had that experience? Or do you think they're just drinking and talking, oblivious to the magic that just happened on stage?"

"I think they're oblivious," Boris hypothesized. Of course, there was no way to know. But I felt so grateful to have had the experience I did and to have shared it with Boris. He looked at me with admiration and reached out to hold my head in his hands as he kissed me.

"I'm so happy right now," I said.

"I'm happy you're happy," he said, smiling.

The blues bar was now my second home too. Being there with him, listening to the blues, I had come home.

I recalled thoughts I'd written in my journal at the age of twenty-five. I'd struggled with feeling like I had no "home." I realized now that home is not a physical structure, not a geographic location, not even a collection of people or belongings. Home is a feeling. And it's within us all, always.

As the musicians exited the stage and were about to make their way through the crowd, Boris excitedly tapped my shoulder. "Look, the guitarist you love so much is coming this way. You should tell him how much you are moved by his music."

"Nawww." I hung back shyly. I have an age-old impulse to reject approaching strangers. I've overcome my shy nature to a large degree in my adulthood, but it still resurfaces from time to time. I find it interesting that those times often include when I feel a deep admiration for someone and know in my heart that it should be expressed. Giving a compliment (when not done in a creepy way) should be the safest way to approach a stranger—don't we all love a bit of sincere flattery? But an unfounded fear often holds me back.

"Go on, he would love to hear from you." Boris gently tried to persuade me.

"No, that's okay." I was persistent.

Boris decided to seize the moment himself. "Hey, man"—he tapped the guitarist on the shoulder to slow his passing—"we really enjoyed your set. You're an incredible guitarist. You claim the position as her favorite." He motioned to me with a smile. I regretted that the words had not come out of my own mouth.

"Wow, thank you. I'm so glad you enjoyed it!" The man's face lit up as he continued creating a path through the crowd with his outstretched guitar case.

Boris made it seem so easy to initiate a conversation with a stranger. Of course, it really is easy, when we let go of fear and come from love. I made a point to continue working on that.

Our decision to stay at the bar until the next live music set was a blessing, as it gave Boris and me a chance to share deeper conversation. By now I'd learned that he was best equipped to open up on a verbally intimate level when he had beer in hand. I listened as he talked about his troubled relationship with his father, how he disliked the responsibility he felt for his mother when she called him her favorite son, and how he had disconnected himself emotionally from his parents as a child, when after their divorce he'd had to divide his time living with each parent. He learned to adjust to being away from one, then the other, until he could be away from both without missing them.

Habit dictated that I respond with sadness to his story, but I knew that it was perfect. Perhaps it contributed to him choosing to live in London and having the richness and depth of experience that stepping outside of one's country and culture allows.

We talked about romantic relationships too.

"All my hair that I've lost...it can be attributed to one girlfriend in particular." Boris laughed but meant what he said. "She was always challenging me. It was good. It wasn't until this last year that I stopped comparing every woman I met to her. I felt that if they weren't as good as her, pursuing a relationship with them would be like taking a step back. They had to have all of her good qualities, but without all the intense fighting. Now I'm able to appreciate the new qualities other women can bring as well. But that relationship taught me a lot."

"I learned a lot from my five years with Sam as well," I shared. "I learned about giving each other grace and offering total acceptance of where the other is at. I can't change anyone else; I can inspire and support them if they want to change, but that's all."

Boris looked at me with appreciation, I believe, appreciation for beauty. When we share our truth and allow our spirit to shine, our beauty cannot be denied. I saw his as well.

I asked him if he'd ever come up with an answer to his ex-girlfriend's question of who he was.

He took a breath and offered, "I can't really put it into words. It's a feeling. I am 'comfortable.' I know who I am, and I'm okay with that."

I'd heard someone's reply to this question at the spiritual retreat: "I am who I am." I love that. We are who we are. The ultimate statement of acceptance.

We returned home after just a few songs. The timing was perfect for a late dinner with the housemates. We heated the meal I'd made the night before and sat down together for what would be the only meal during my whole trip that all four of us would share. We visited for a while after the meal, before Alex and Jakub went up to their rooms. Boris and I remained at the table for what was probably another two hours. I mostly just listened, as the wine at dinner loosened Boris's tongue even more. The more he talked, the more of his soul I got to know.

He put on some background music for us to enjoy.

"This is Chopin's Funeral March. I love this piece of music. It's the third movement of his Piano Sonata No. 2 in B-flat minor."

What? Was this the same punk rocker I'd met in Argentina? I marveled at the number of times he'd revealed a side of himself I would never have imagined existed.

As we finally made our way up to the bedroom after midnight, the soul connection we'd been cultivating proceeded to offer me the longest and most incredible lovemaking session I'd ever experienced in my life. The duration and attention Boris gifted my body led me to experience such an intense circulation of energy in my hands and arms that I was moved to laughter.

"Feel my hands! Can you *feel* that?" I was sure he would electrocute himself when he touched them. I wondered if this was what "everyone else" usually experienced, and I was simply late in the game. I didn't care, though—it was incredible! Something released in me emotionally. I asked how he could possibly last this long.

"I don't, usually, but I want it to last with you. I could stay inside you all night."

I melted. For all I knew, he said that to everyone he brought home. But I didn't think so. I sat up, my legs on either side of Boris's body.

"Let's breathe each other's breath," he suggested. "It's something in the *Kama Sutra*. The *Kama Sutra* is much more than just positions—it's about partnership."

I was open to anything. We shared each other's life force in partnership.

We laid back, still joined together, in ecstasy.

"I can't believe it—after all these years I am inside of you again," he shared.

I was moved to tears. It was the first time that I'd cried from joy while making love. I was so overcome with gratitude. Had he asked, I don't think I would have even been able to describe what I was feeling. I simply knew I felt alive.

"You deserve the best," he whispered, stroking my body from the base of my spine to the back of my shoulders, and my body tingled with sensation.

I now knew what "the best" could feel like. I knew it was possible for me. It was hard to believe that just one and a half years ago, I sat in a group of women and shared that I preferred chocolate over sex. That, in fact, I could do without sex entirely. And now here I was, not only desiring it but relishing it. Every pore of my being called out for it. I *was* a sexual being—a "real" woman. *Thank you, thank you, thank you,* my spirit called out. I wasn't damaged after all—I was whole. I had been all along.

The night ended with Boris leading me to lie on my side facing the opposite wall. He took me in, stroking my back, butt, and thighs, so gently and tenderly, for what felt like an hour. Where did this guy come from? Can we get more of them, please? Perhaps many women are accustomed to this experience, but after listening to the women in my therapy groups, I sadly know that many are not.

For years, I had fantasized about experiencing ecstasy—the divine connection among mind, body, and spirit in unity with a partner, without shame or fear. I realized, lying up against Boris's body, that my fantasy had just come true.

28
Coming Full Circle

Days 11-12

I indulged in a slow morning on Monday. Everyone was at work, the peacefulness of the house was reflective of my mood. It was my last day in London. I had not felt like a tourist; there were no attractions I had planned to see or needed to cram in. I had simply wanted to experience "a day in the life" of Boris, twelve times over. I felt I had succeeded in that.

You could say I'd traveled to visit a friend—that's what I'd told most everybody. But Boris was more than a friend. Yes, he was a lover, but he was more than that too. He was a symbol of the ultimate fantasy. My experience in Buenos Aires was not terribly unique, but it was essential to my identity. My memory of Boris stood for something. It was proof that I had *lived.* I wanted to reach out for that feeling again—for that fantasy—without having to know where it would lead me. I simply knew that it would be worth it.

My trip to London had pulsed in my veins since I saw Boris on video chat again back in November. He was a reminder of what was missing in my life. The dream, the fantasy. My soul cried out for that. I needed to know that he was real. Because if he was real, the fantasy could be real too. And if I could share with him who I'd become, I would have come full circle. He'd be a witness to my journey. I had the opportunity to show one man, at least, before and after snapshots of a significant era in my life. We so often don't notice the changes in a person when we're next to that person on the journey. So here was a unique opportunity to reveal to another my sexual healing, my spiritual discovery, my inner essence.

I considered my journey over the past nearly two weeks as I left Boris's house to walk through the nearby Southwark Park, all the way to Tower Bridge downtown. I stopped at a coffee shop and journaled in reflection. I wrote him a letter I would later leave for him. I observed the city and bid it farewell while waiting for Boris to finish his work day. I had asked him to meet me at a particular intersection for dinner, without telling him our destination.

At the intersection, he snuck up on me outside the restaurant one last time, while I was looking another direction. He grabbed my arm to lead me down the street.

"Wait!" I called out, "It's here!" He had not noticed the sign: *Constancia Argentine Grill*. He laughed, and we went inside.

It took a while for Boris to come down off his work day. The atmosphere was still tense at the office, and he was still confused as to what his next steps should be. I listened patiently before finally interjecting, "Boris, let's just enjoy the evening."

I watched the glow of his eyes change from that of mild stress to calm presence.

"You're right. I'm done talking about work."

We reached across the candlelit table and held hands.

I wondered if he'd noticed the subtleties of the moment. Tango music played in the background. We were listening to Spanish, sharing empanadas, ice cream, and a bottle of wine. We had come full circle.

Back at his place, I attempted to casually pack my belongings, without dwelling on what the act signified. It didn't take me long, and I rejoined Boris in his room for the night. He was sitting on his bed, playing guitar. I took a seat facing him on the floor. I wanted to watch him play one last time; I could see the transfer of emotion from his soul to the synapses in his brain, culminating in euphoric release through his fingertips. It was divine.

He began to play "Love Hurts," before stopping to ask me if I'd heard the version performed by Norah Jones and Keith Richards. I had not. He pulled up the video on his laptop, and together in the dark we watched their chemistry unfold onscreen. My own body responded with a chemical mixture of pleasure and pain as I absorbed the lyrics.

The final notes trailed off as Boris turned to me.

"It's beautiful, isn't it?"

I answered yes, but I'd wanted to say so much more. What was it about the song that moved him? What was he feeling?

Instead, I turned to the logistics of my final night. I returned his phone and T-shirt and gave him the book I had bought him; he read the note I'd written on the inside cover. He thanked me and hugged me, and I fought the anxiety of feeling like there was so much more I could have written, so much more to say…

We didn't go to sleep that night. We lay in his bed, holding each other. I broke the silence to say something

I'd wanted to say in person for several months. I took a deep breath. After all the spiritual practice I'd done on speaking my truth, it was still not easy for me to say.

"So many people are afraid to say I love you, because instantly they worry that they won't hear it back. And if they do, they begin to worry that they'll lose it."

Boris nodded nervously.

"But I want to say now, without needing to hear anything in return, and without any expectation for where it might lead, that I love you."

He turned toward me, held my face, and kissed my forehead before lying back and staring at the ceiling. I saw a tear start streaming down his cheek, then another.

"Why are you crying?" I asked. He didn't answer. "It's beautiful," I stated, giving him the opportunity to not have my question hang in the air. I could tell he wasn't ready to answer it.

After a few more moments of silence, he started. "Sometimes I find myself wanting someone to share…to dedicate myself to. Sometimes I can picture myself with someone…it's so close I can feel it." His sentence was somewhat broken. I couldn't be completely sure of the interpretation, but I gauged that he just might be picturing me. I think he was afraid to express it directly, as to do so would only bring about that heavy, unspoken question that neither of us was prepared to answer: *What next?* But he continued, "There are so few women that intrigue me enough to want to commit to long-term. You are one of those people who I want to try being with 100 percent."

"Do you remember the scene from *Before Sunset*?" I asked. "Jesse asks Celine why they didn't exchange phone numbers, and she answers it was because they were young and didn't yet realize that such deep connections only happen a few times in life. I don't ever want to forget that."

Boris remained silent. He was still crying. He then sat up. "Before, I was okay. Then you came, and you shook my mind and my heart."

I wondered if that was a good thing.

"It's good." He smiled and kissed me. He had read my mind.

"Were you happy before? From your soul, were you happy?" I asked.

"I was happy…" He seemed to trail off.

"Then you don't have to change anything," I offered.

"But I still feel unfulfilled." He finished with his own words.

He spoke his truth. I hoped I had helped to break up some energy that might lead him on the path towards fulfillment—not necessarily with me, but within himself.

He sighed. "I regret not going to Paris with you." He leaned over to me and rested his head on my chest. "I am so sorry," he added, his tears becoming heavier now.

I wrapped my arm around his neck and cradled his head. "London was perfect; everything was perfect," I responded. He continued to weep. I was so touched. He trusted me with his tears, with his vulnerability. What a miraculous gift I was being given.

We didn't say much more that night. We pressed our bodies up against each other and entwined our feet. We were searching for every point of contact possible. My head in his hands, he whispered with longing, "My girl, my girl." They were the sweetest words I'd ever heard. I understood that they were words of affection, not possession. In that moment, I wanted to be nothing more than his girl. In fact, in the divine measure of time as simply here and now, that's all I really was. I offered all of me to him in that moment.

I recall now the strict aversion to being called a girl that I'd had back in Buenos Aires; I'd wanted so badly to be a woman. But now, I understand that we are a composite of the spirit of both child and adult and that when releasing our inner child, those are the moments when we're often the most beautiful—and the most wise.

It was now probably 2:00 a.m. Boris dozed off on occasion but woke fully at 4:00 a.m. He knew I was still awake. He cradled the length of my body and again caressed my foot with his own. His arm reached around to my belly, and he stroked beneath my shirt. His hand swept around my waist and lowered to my bottom. He pulled me in tighter to him; his breathing got heavier. My eyes were closed; my heart sped up to keep pace with his. One last time. We explored and entered each other's bodies in gratitude and farewell.

My alarm was not to go off until 6:00 a.m. For the remainder of the time, we lay in bed, holding each other.

"I'm going with you to the airport," he said with conviction.

"You are?" I said, surprised. He had to work that day yet; I had not expected him to accompany me.

"Yes, I have time to go there and still get to work."

"Thank you." I was truly grateful.

"There's a song by Robert Johnson," he said thoughtfully. "Can I play it for you?"

He reached for his phone.

"It's called 'Love in Vain,' but, well, I don't think it's in vain." He pressed play, as the lyrics caressed our naked bodies like a lullaby, harkening of the agony of following one's love to the train station before having to part ways.

The song ended just as the alarm went off. Our bodies went through the motions of showering, dressing, and collecting my luggage to walk to the tube station. It was a gorgeous morning; the sun was peaking over the horizon, its reflection dancing with the ripples of water in the canal outside his home. I took in the scene that I'd witnessed only in photos months before. I was not yet prepared to return to seeing this view of his world through mere images again.

We had over an hour to pass on the tube. We sat close together, cradling my luggage and each other. I tried to memorize the subtleties of his touch.

We arrived at Heathrow Terminal 3 and checked my luggage. Boris marveled again at the weight of what I carried. We had breakfast together in silence, stealing glances at each other on occasion. Eventually, Boris looked at his watch. 8:40 a.m.

"It's time." He sighed with remorse.

We rose and headed toward security. We stopped by a wide column, using it as an obstruction for privacy. Boris set down his work bag, grabbed me, and planted one of those Latin kisses on my trembling lips. Oh, how I'd miss those kisses.

"I'm going to miss you," he spoke. "I wish I had more time to spend with you."

"Me too," I agreed. "It won't be six years before we see each other again," I offered. My breathing was getting heavy with anxiety.

Boris shook his head incredulously, "No. I'll look into coming to Portland."

I wondered if we were making empty promises, to ease the discomfort of saying goodbye. How could we really promise these things? We'd allowed life to keep us apart for six years, after all.

"That would be so nice." I wanted to believe in the fantasy again. I reminded myself that we needed merely to decide to see each other again. We'd know when it was time. We embraced. Releasing the embrace, our hands still held each other's.

He gave a final squeeze. "Go, fast." He looked away.

I squeezed back, grabbed my shoulder bag, and headed to the security line. My mind was not present, and I had trouble scanning my boarding ticket. The airport attendant reluctantly came over to help me.

I turned to see Boris walking the length of the rope. We simultaneously blew each other a kiss. This was how we would end our video calls. "*Besos,*" I whispered, and I saw him do the same. This was it. We'd be back in each other's virtual worlds after this, wondering if the other were "real" again—if the intensity of this feeling were real or simply imagined.

I made my way through security and stopped in a gift shop. It was the last place where London souvenirs would be available, and I'd been wanting to buy something for my nephew. I saw a rack of teddy bears with London skyline T-shirts on. I stood looking at the skyline, for I don't know how long.

"Ma'am, are you all right?" The salesclerk had approached me from behind.

"Yes," I jumped. "Yes, I'm all right."

"We have some very nice bears over her too. It's a better deal, for a bigger bear."

"Thank you." I smiled.

I bought the bigger bear. It could also serve as a pillow on my long flight back.

Now, I wonder if the bear was more for my nephew or more for me. I hugged the bear to my chest and went to wait at my gate.

Taking a seat by the window, I gazed out at the sky, watching the clouds slowly shift shapes.

"Back to just you and me, God," I whispered out loud. How beautiful, that we can never truly be lonely—because we're never truly alone.

I pulled out my iPod and put on my headphones. I needed to hear some blues. I sank back farther into my seat and allowed Eva Cassidy's "Stormy Monday" to once again sooth my soul.

I closed my eyes and smiled sweetly.

Mmmm. Home.

Epilogue

THROUGHOUT MY ADULT life, with each international journey or new romance that I embark on and divulge to friends or blog readers, I repeatedly find myself on the receiving end of the comment, "I am vicariously living through you." Though I am humbled that others find my storytelling and life adventures to be worthy of escaping within, my real desire is to inspire everyone to live his or her *own* life, to the fullest and highest degree possible.

Please, dear reader, do not take what I have written as a declaration of truth. Rather, search within yourself to discover what resonates with you as your own truth. I do not know where your soul is trying to go—so I cannot declare if what is true for me is true for you.

The story you have just read is but a snapshot of one person's journey toward discovering her own truth. There are many more stories, and many more truths, to be told. So, if you find yourself wondering, "What happens next?" in this story, allow me to point out that the real question is:

What happens next in *your* story?

Look back at your own story; what beliefs are you hanging on to that no longer serve your soul? What is holding you back from experiencing the most magnificent version of yourself that you could possibly imagine? What would you do—who would you be—if you knew you couldn't fail?

Can you go back and consider the experiences that you've had as, perhaps, absolutely perfect? That without them, you wouldn't be the person you are today—this incredible being, willing and able to step beyond your past and into the unfamiliar, knowing that what lies beyond will be scary and challenging but worth it, beyond even your wildest fantasy?

From my experience, I've learned that finding ecstasy first lies in the belief that you always have a choice as to how you want to react to any given circumstance and, therefore, how you want to experience your own life. Second, ecstasy lies in the belief that you are worthy of love—releasing the fear and expectation of needing to be loved by another and simply loving yourself. Third, ecstasy lies in the courage to be vulnerable.

Are you willing to accept that there are no victims or villains? People who present themselves in this world as what we would call villains are simply taking the fastest path toward remembering who they are—and offering a context in which we can respond and remember who we are. Our soul has always known, but our human existence demands that we learn by experience. We cannot be victims, because that word implies that we have no free choice as to how we respond to what happens to us, nor that what happens to us is actually a great lesson and opportunity for our true being to spring forth in all its glory.

Are you willing to do everything it takes to completely and unconditionally love yourself? If this is something you struggle with, there are so many resources available to help you on your path. Visit the library, research therapy groups or counselors specific to your struggle, put yourself out there. Start talking. Buy a Magic Wand.

Are you willing to be vulnerable? Imagine if you shared your biggest shame, your deepest fears, your highest truth. If you're already naked, what then would you have to lose?

If you own your story, you get to write its ending.

Of course, no story ever truly ends, for "the end" is merely another way to say "a new beginning." There's always something that happens next.

So, what happens next in your story?

Acknowledgments

I NEVER PLANNED to write this book. It just happened to me. Or rather, it happened *through* me, after a good friend suggested that I tell the story of my sexual transformation. My initial reaction was that I couldn't possibly share details of my sex life with the world—I mean, my *parents* would read it!

But the seed had been planted and was further nurtured the following day when I received an e-mail that began, "Dear Rebecca: Have you ever thought about writing a book?" and continued on to announce Christine Kloser's Transformational Author Experience program and writing contest. I took it as a sign from the Universe. Almost instantly I knew my world was about to change. I realized I could use my story to help others who are struggling with sexual repression and shame to live fuller lives.

Once the decision was made to share my story, the words poured out of me. I suddenly discovered that I had *a lot* to say—and the fact that the subject matter was so personal and often taboo to talk about was exactly the reason I needed to say it (my parents' reaction notwithstanding).

What I was humbled to discover, however, was that not only did my parents offer their unwavering support but so did everyone else who played a part in my journey and would appear in the book. The transformation that takes place in this story has only been the beginning—writing the story, sharing it with friends, family, and former lovers, and then sharing it with the world have each been powerfully transformative experiences of their own. All names have been changed for anonymity, but you know who you are. Thank you, from the bottom of my heart. It means so much to me.

I also extend my deepest gratitude to those who have been beautiful sources of love and support throughout the writing and publishing process. To Julie Vaillancourt, Erica Schoenborn, Amy McMackin, Jesse Olson, Ashley Cline, Jess Gibson, Heather Weidman, Jenn Fowler and Juniper Vojta for being the first to read my initial drafts and offer the encouragement and motivation to keep going—your belief in me and this story has been crucial to my commitment to stay on this wild ride!

Thank you to all of the official editors that contributed to making this book what it has become—Kristin Thiel, Marlene Oulton, Maya Seaman, and Amy Botula.

And last but certainly not least, thank you to my mentors: to Christine Kloser, "The Transformation Catalyst," for making it impossible for me to ignore my calling, and to Neale Donald Walsh for having the courage to publish your own truth, no matter how controversial it may be. By doing so, you have improved the lives of millions.

To all of the aforementioned individuals, this really isn't "my" book. It is *ours*. And now, dear reader, it is also *yours*. Thank you for taking this journey with me.

Finding Ecstasy
Discussion Guide

FINDING ECSTASY TOUCHES on many interpretations of sexuality and spirituality that can be used as a guide to further explore your own beliefs. Below are some questions to ask yourself and to perhaps discuss within a group. You may also wish to explore these topics in writing or to sit with questions and return to them later when you are most connected to your feelings about a particular topic. Remember, there are no "right" or "wrong" answers, only what feels true for you.

SEXUALITY AND RELATIONSHIPS

1. Look back on your own childhood and adolescence. How did the messages you received from your family, spiritual community, teachers, etc. affect how you've viewed your own sexuality? Are your current beliefs a product of these influences, or do you believe you can determine for yourself what is "right" or "wrong" for you in regards to sex and relationships?

2. Can you think of other beliefs about who you are that might be a result of influences outside of yourself? Do these beliefs currently serve you?

3. Do you believe that the sex education and health instruction you received in school thoroughly and fairly represented multiple sides of each issue? How could they be improved upon?

4. Do you think you're responsible for your own sexual pleasure? Or is it your partner's responsibility?

5. Have you ever had an experience where someone in a position of authority expected you to say or do something that you knew in your heart did not feel right for you? What did you do about it?

6. Do you believe it's possible to maintain friendships with former lovers? What do you think reconnecting with your past lovers today would be like? What do you think their perspectives of your relationships or experiences would be?

7. Have there been incidences in your life where you've felt like a fraud? If you still feel this way, what would it take to shift that belief?

8. Do you believe that irregularities or discomfort in our bodies are warning signs that there's something larger we need to pay attention to? Are our emotions and beliefs about ourselves linked to our physical health?

9. How do you define the word *vulnerable*? What feelings come up for you when you hear the word *vulnerability*? Do you think it's important to be vulnerable in relationships?

10. Have you stayed in a relationship too long? Where do you think the line is between putting the necessary work into a relationship or gracefully letting your partner go?

11. Do you agree with the idea that most people enter into relationships with an eye toward what they can get out of them rather than put into them? What are the reasons you have entered into relationships?

12. Do you agree that love-sponsored action is first what produces the highest good for *you*—and that what is best for you becomes what is best for another? Why or why not?

13. Do you believe that we are in need of no *particular* other in order to be whole and complete—but that we need *another* to know who we are? Has your happiness ever felt fully dependent on a particular other?

14. How has your relationship with your parents evolved from childhood to adulthood? Are you able to be more authentic with them as an adult? Do you no longer fight about things you used to fight about?

SPIRITUALITY

15. Do you believe in the source commonly referred to as God (the Universe, etc.)? If so, do you believe this source is separate from you or part of you? Why?

16. Do you or could you believe in a God who says there is no right or wrong? No judgment or condemnation? No absolute truth? If so, what impact would this have on your life and the world?

17. Do you believe you have to have things in order to do

things in order to be something? Or could it be possible that the reverse is a greater truth? Try it for yourself—be what you seek to have and see what happens.

18. Think about a recent experience that you found unpleasant. Can you reflect back on how you may have reacted to the same experience so that you would have experienced it as positive?

19. Do you believe that the soul never dies—and that it chooses when to leave a particular body or life experience? How does or would this belief change the way you view death?

20. Do you agree that everything comes from either love or fear? What are some current situations in your life that you believe come from fear? What would love do, instead?

21. What are aspects of your life that you feel shame around? What would it take to release them? What do you think the result of sharing your truths would be? What's the worst that could happen? And then what? Keep going with that list until your fear dissipates.

22. Do you believe that we merely need to decide something in order for it to happen? That the "how" works itself out, once we fully commit to that decision?

23. What is your relationship to the question, "What do you do?" Do you believe that your job defines you? Catch yourself the next time you find yourself about to ask

someone this question and instead ask, "What brings you joy?" or "What would you do if you knew you couldn't fail?"

24. Who are you? Try this exercise: List ten answers to this question, then cross off three, then three more, then three more, until you're left with only one. Which were the hardest parts of your identity to cross off?

25. Keep a gratitude journal for forty days. Remember also to offer gratitude for the things you're *least* grateful for, without trying to figure out why you could be grateful for them. Also offer gratitude for things you desire, as if you already have them, and see what happens.

26. Do you believe that there are no victims or villains, only messengers meant to show us who we are in relationship to them? When you hear the perspective that Hitler was not a villain, what comes up for you?

27. When have you held your energy back from its natural flow? Do you think, as an adult, that you can rediscover the innocence of childhood—to play in the sand (without a child present), to "dance so someone watches"?

28. How would your world change if you consistently told yourself at the sign of adversity, "This problem has already been solved for me"? Can you look back on the tapestry of your own life and see that it is perfect?

Further Reading

Join the *Finding Ecstasy* newsletter list at *www.findingecstasy.com* for bonus materials, inspirational musings, and giveaways!

Conversations with God: An Uncommon Dialogue
Neale Donald Walsh

The Way of the Peaceful Warrior: A Book That Changes Lives
Dan Millman

Women's Bodies, Women's Wisdom: Creating Physical and Emotional Health and Healing
Dr. Christiane Northrup

Taking Charge of your Fertility: The Definitive Guide to Natural Birth Control and Pregnancy Achievement
Toni Weschler

Sex for One: The Joy of Selfloving
Betty Dodson

Becoming Orgasmic: A Sexual and Personal Growth Program for Women
Julia Heiman

The Passion Prescription: Ten Weeks to Your Best Sex—Ever!
Laura Berman

The Seven Principles for Making Marriage Work
John M. Gottman

Make Miracles in 40 Days: Turning What You Have into What You Want
Melody Beattie

Outwitting the Devil: The Secret to Freedom and Success
Napoleon Hill

Resources and Charities

JULIE JESKE SEX THERAPY

Julie is an Individual and Couples Counselor who helps clients increase intimacy, passion, sexual satisfaction and pleasure with themselves and/or their partner. Online courses and self-study guides available.
www.juliejeske.com

LIVING YOGA

Living Yoga is a nonprofit outreach program based in Portland, Oregon that teaches yoga as a tool for personal change in prisons, drug and alcohol rehabilitation centers, and transitional facilities.
www.living-yoga.org

BIG BROTHERS BIG SISTERS

Big Brothers Big Sisters helps at-risk children realize their potential by providing them with one-to-one relationships with adult mentors.
www.bbbs.org

About the Author

THOUGH ONE OF her childhood fantasies was to have superhuman powers that allowed her to travel instantaneously around the globe—or at the very least, fly—it is Rebecca's distinctly human persona that causes strangers and dogs alike to want to be her new best friend. With a commitment to spreading joy and inspiring others to let go of shame and let shine their light, Rebecca unabashedly reveals her own vulnerability so that others may feel safe exploring their own.

Rebecca was a prize winner in Christine Kloser's 2013 Transformational Author Writing Contest and has been featured on Viki Winterton's *Write Now Radio!* program alongside top literary experts and publishing professionals. She currently resides in the Pacific Northwest, though you may not find her there year-round—a vagabond spirit cannot be tamed. You could look for her frolicking in forests or careening on rocks by the sea, but you'll have a better chance following her at www.duendepressbooks.com.

www.ingramcontent.com/pod-product-compliance
Lightning Source LLC
Chambersburg PA
CBHW022003090426
42741CB00007B/873
* 9 7 8 0 9 9 1 5 2 5 4 1 6 *